W9-BWE-515

Using Copyrighted

Videocassettes

COPYRIGHT INFORMATION BULLETIN SERIES:

1. Jerome K. Miller, *Using Copyrighted Videocasssettes in Classrooms and Libraries*, 1984 (out of print).

2. Charles W. Vlcek, *Copyright Policy Development: A Resource Book for Educators*, 1987.

3. Jerome K. Miller, *Using Copyrighted Videocasssettes in Classrooms, Libraries, and Training Centers*, Second edition, 1988.

4. Esther R. Sinofsky, *A Copyright Primer For Educational and Industrial Media Producers.*, 1988.

5. Jerome K. Miller (Ed.), *Video Copyright Permissions*, (scheduled for 1988).

Using Copyrighted Videocassettes in Classrooms, Libraries, and Training Centers

SECOND EDITION

by

Dr. Jerome K. Miller

COPYRIGHT INFORMATION SERVICES

Copyright Information Bulletin No. 3

Copyright, 1984, 1988, Copyright Information Services
All Rights Reserved

First edition titled: Using Copyrighted Videocassettes in
Classrooms and Libraries

Copying in excess of fair use
requires paying clearance fees to the:

Copyright Clearance Center (CCC)
21 Congress St., Salem, MA 01970

CCC: 0-914143-14-X/$00.00 + $1.00

Published and distributed by:
COPYRIGHT INFORMATION SERVICES
Post Office Box 1460
Friday Harbor, WA 98250

Library of Congress Cataloging-in-Publication Data

Miller, Jerome K.
    Using copyrighted videocassettes in classrooms,
libraries, and training centers.

    (Copyright information bulletin ; no. 3)
    Rev. ed. of: Using copyrighted videocassettes in
classrooms and libraries. c1984.
    Bibliography: p.
    Includes index.
    1. Video recording--Fair use (Copyright)--United
States. I. Miller, Jerome K. (Using copyrighted
videocassettes in classrooms and libraries. II. Titl
III. Series.
KF3030.4.M54   1987   346.7304'82   87-24572
ISBN 0-914143-14-X   347.306482

DISCLAIMER

The opinions contained herein
reflect the author's informed opinion,
but do not constitute legal advice.

DEDICATION

to Prof. Lawrence W.S. Auld

No truer friend could be imagined.

INTRODUCTION TO THE FIRST EDITION

Through my consulting practice, I receive many calls from educators and librarians who are concerned about the legality of using copyrighted videocassettes in classrooms or in library viewing rooms, carrels, or auditoriums. Many callers tell me they received a written warning from the Film Security Office of the Motion Picture Association of America (MPAA) and they wonder if it affects their educational or library services. The MPAA warning notice was distributed to schools, colleges, and libraries by film companies in an effort to stop illegal performances. The opening lines of the notice read:

WARNING

"FOR HOME USE ONLY" MEANS JUST THAT!

BY LAW, as well as by intent, the pre-recorded video cassettes and video-discs available in stores throughout the United States are FOR HOME USE ONLY.[1]

The notice continues with a statement of the proprietors' exclusive right to regulate performances of videocassettes. Educators and librarians who receive the warning notice frequently express concern about a key statement in the notice:

"[P]erformances in 'semipublic' places such as clubs, lodges, factories, summer camps, and schools are 'public performances' subject to copyright control."[2] Educators seeing "school" in the quotation fear it denies the right to perform videocassettes in classrooms, while librarians wonder if libraries also fall under the ban on performances in public or semipublic places. The answers to these questions aren't always simple — and some inquirers are sure to be displeased with my response. Nonetheless, I hope this book will be useful to its intended audience.

A few educators and librarians call me to inquire about the "Home-Use-Only" warning labels on videocassettes. They frequently wonder if the labels are binding on their institutions. There appears to be little doubt these warning labels are advisory only, and do not affect the purchaser's performance rights—as great or limited as they may be.

This book does not treat the duplication of copyrighted videocassettes, as that topic has been covered in my earlier works, and the works of others. The topic does not appear to require redefinition at present, although that situation could change at any time.

INTRODUCTION TO THE SECOND EDITION

The first edition of this book was kindly received by its intended audience—educators and librarians who are responsible for video performances in their workplaces. After exhausting two printings, the first edition was allow to go out of print, so it could be replaced by a revised edition reflecting recent legal history. Since the appearance of the first edition, the federal appeals court sustained the lower court in *Columbia Pictures* v. *Redd Horne*. The decision was not unexpected and appears to sustain the proprietors' right to control public performances of films and videocassettes. A similar case, *Columbia Pictures* v. *Aveco*, commonly called the Nickelodeon case, was heard in federal district and appellate courts and reached a similar decision. Since the first edition was written, educators and librarians have shown an increasing concern about public performances of videocassettes. MGM/UA discontinued its licensing service to nonprofit agencies and turned that service over to another firm. Several firms now license video performances in public libraries, on college and university campuses, and elsewhere. The treatment of video performances in public libraries has been expanded to reflect the performance right advocacy role assumed by the American Library Association.

At the request of several readers, the treatment of video performances in churches and hospitals has been expanded and moved to a new chapter. The new chapter also treats performing videocassettes in industrial training centers. Another new chapter begins to address video performance rights in business meetings.

As before, the issue of videotaping off the air has been omitted as it is satisfactorily treated in other publications.[1] Likewise, this book does not address the issue of duplicating video recordings, as that issue is beyond the scope of this book.

ACKNOWLEDGMENTS TO THE FIRST EDITION

Thanks are due to many who contributed to the preparation of this book. Robert Wedgeworth, Executive Director of the American Library Association, granted permission to quote from Newton N. Minow's letter about using videodiscs in libraries. Burton H. Hanft supplied copies of court documents and a written response to Mr. Minnow's comments. Stuart Snyder, of MGM/UA, and Joan Powell and Michael Garofalo, of the Los Angeles County Public Library, supplied information about the MGM/UA performance license. Walter C. Allen read the manuscript and offered helpful comments for its improvement. My thanks to each one for their generous assistance.

Finally, my sister, Mrs. T.H. Pepin, has been a constant source of encouragement in getting this book published, and in many other ways.

ACKNOWLEDGEMENTS TO THE SECOND EDITION

In addition to the individuals named above, I would like to acknowledge the help of many educators and librarians who supplied information about licenses they have acquired, or about the proprietors' efforts to force them to stop performing videocassettes. Thanks are also due to representatives of several firms who supplied information about their licenses and their efforts to license video performances. Thanks are also due to Prof. Lawrence W.S. Auld for reading the manuscript and making suggestions for its improvement. This book is dedicated to him.

TABLE OF CONTENTS

KEY TERMINOLOGY

Every discipline develops a unique vocabulary which aids the specialist but confounds the novice. The legal profession is a prime example of this linguistic phenomenon, so those who want to understand copyright must grapple with its vocabulary. This book uses two common words which have unique meanings in the copyright law:

To "display" a work means . . . in the case of a motion picture or other audiovisual work, to show individual images nonsequentially.[1]

To "perform" a work means . . . in the case of a motion picture or other audiovisual work, to show its images in any sequence or to make the sounds accompanying it audible.[2]

The terms videotape, videocassette, and videodisc are specific technical terms, but for simplicity, this book uses videocassette as a generic term covering all three items. Videocassette, videotape, and videodisc do not appear to have unique meanings in the law.

CHAPTER I:

PROPRIETORS' RIGHTS

Statutory copyright law was created 277 years ago to protect authors' rights. It has been revised many times since, but its purpose remains essentially unchanged. The Copyright Revision Act of 1976 implemented this purpose by giving authors, including film and video producers, substantial control over various uses of their creative works:

Sect. 106. Exclusive rights in copyrighted works.

Subject to sections 107 through 118, the owner of copyright under this title has the exclusive rights to do and to authorize any of the following:

(1) to reproduce the copyrighted work in copies or phonorecords;

(2) to prepare derivative works based upon the copyrighted work;

(3) to distribute copies or phonorecords of the copyrighted work to the public by sale or other transfer of ownership, or by rental, lease, or lending;

(4) in the case of literary, musical, dramatic, and choreographic works, pantomimes, and motion pictures and other audiovisual works, to perform the copyrighted work publicly; and

(5) in the case of literary, musical, dramatic, and choreographic works, pantomimes, and pictorial, graphic, or sculptural works, including the individual images of a motion picture or other audiovisual work, to display the copyrighted work publicly.[1]

The first right restricts printing and other reproductions. The second right gives proprietors control over derivative works, such as new editions of books, films based on books, and clothing and posters displaying cartoon characters. The third right, the "right of first publication," gives proprietors the right to keep products off the market. However, this right expires when the work legitimately enters the market—through sale, lease, or lending.

The fourth right is the central issue of this book. It enables proprietors to maintain artistic control and secure income from performances of their copyrighted works. The fifth right provides a similar control on displays of copyrighted art works.

When the copyright act was revised in 1976, the for-profit-performance-in-public limitation in the 1909 act was replaced with subsections four and five, described above. Although the new act enhanced the proprietors' right to control performances and displays, the act also authorized certain performances and displays without permission or fees. Some of these exemptions are treated in this book. Congress could not resolve every issue raised by the Copyright Revision Act, so many points were left for the courts to resolve. The courts were soon asked to draw a dividing line between public and private performances in *Columbia Pictures* v. *Redd Horne*.

COLUMBIA PICTURES V. REDD HORNE

The case centers on innovative business practices employed at two Erie, PA video stores, Maxwell's Video Showcase and Maxwell's Video Showcase East. The stores, hereafter Maxwell's, were owned and managed by Redd Horne Inc., and operated by Glenn W. Zeny, the president of Redd Horne. His brother, Robert Zeny, managed the stores. The stores sold and rented video equipment and prerecorded videocassettes; they also sold blank videocassettes. The sale and rental of equipment and prerecorded cassettes and the sale of blank cassettes are legitimate services which were excluded from the plaintiffs' complaint.

Each store had over forty private video viewing booths. Each booth was carpeted and equipped with a nineteen-inch, color television set and comfortable benches for two to four viewers. The television sets were wired to videocassette players located behind the counters, in the front of the stores. The exteriors of the stores had theater-like marquees and theater-like posters were posted in the showrooms. Advertisements for popular films appeared in the theater section of the local newspapers and were broadcast on local radio stations. Clients could choose from numerous film titles, pay a five to eight dollar fee, and see the film in the privacy of a booth. Free popcorn and soft drinks were available to viewers.

Several film companies attempted to stop the practice or license it, but the Zenys insisted that films performed in their "showcasing" service were "private performances" which did not require licenses. When negotiations with the Zenys were unsuccessful, seven film companies (Columbia, Embassy, Paramount, Twentieth Century-Fox, Universal, Disney, and Warner Bros.) filed a complaint against the stores (Maxwell's), the parent firm (Redd Horne), and the Zeny brothers.

The case was heard in the Federal District Court for the Western District of Pennsylvania, in Erie. On July 28, 1983, the court granted the plaintiffs petition for summary judgment.[2] The court later awarded damages of $44,750, plus the plaintiffs' court costs and legal fees.[3]

The Third Circuit Court of Appeals heard the case early in 1985. The Appeals Court decision upheld the lower court decision and rejected the claim that the studios' actions were in constraint of trade. Several key points about place and public accessibility were made in the Appeals Court decision:

The . . . question is whether these performances are public. Section 101 also states that to perform a work "publicly" means "[t]o perform . . . it at a place open to the public or at any place where a substantial number of persons outside of a normal circle of a family and its social acquaintances is gathered. The statute is written in the disjunctive, and thus two categories of places can satisfy the definition of "to perform a work publicly." The first category is self-evident; it is "a place open to the public." The second category, commonly referred to as a semi-public place, is determined by the size and composition of the audience.

The legislative history indicates that this second category was added to expand the concept of public performance by including those places that, although not open to the public at large, are accessible to a significant number of people. Clearly if a place is public, the size and composition of the audience are irrelevant. However, if the place is not public, the size and composition of the audience will be determinative.

We find it unnecessary to examine the second part of the statutory definition because we agree with the district court's conclusion that Maxwell's was open to the public. On the composition of the audience, the district court noted that "the showcasing operation is not distinguishable in any significant manner from the exhibition of films at a conventional movie theater." Any member of the public can view a motion picture by paying the appropriate fee. The services provided by Maxwell's are essentially the same as a movie theater, with the additional feature of privacy. The relevant "place" within the meaning of section 101 is each of Maxwell's two stores, not each individual booth within each store. Simply because the cassettes can be viewed in private does not mitigate the essential fact that Maxwell's is unquestionably open to the public.[4]

COLUMBIA PICTURES V. AVECO

The Redd Horne case was followed by a similar case, *Columbia Pictures* v. *Aveco*, brought by an almost identical group of plaintiffs (Columbia, Embassy, MGM/UA, United, Paramount, Twentieth Century, Universal, Disney, and Warner Bros.). The defendant, Aveco, Inc., did business as Nickelodeon Video Showcase and American Video Exchange. (This is usually called the Nickelodeon case.) The three firms (Aveco, Nickelodeon, and American Video Exchange) and John P. Leonardos were named in the complaint. Nickelodeon operated video theaters in Lock Haven and State College, PA. Each store included viewing rooms seating two to twenty-five persons. Each room had a color television receiver and a videocassette recorder controlled by the persons in the room. The rooms and videocassettes were rented separately; patrons could rent a videocassette and a room for a viewing or they could rent a videocassette for home use, or they could rent a room to view videocassettes obtained from another source. The case was limited to renting a videocassette for viewing at the Nickelodeon. The decision was based in large part on the Redd Horne decision. In addressing the differences in the two cases, the court rejected arguments that there was no difference between renting videocassette for home use and building-use rentals:

> Although there is some superficial appeal to the Defendants' argument that operation of the Nickelodeon is legally indistinguishable from the concededly legal rental of cassettes to customers for home viewing, this argument has no merit. The Nickelodeon clearly offers a service quite different from the service offered by a store that engages in rental of video cassettes alone. The Nickelodeon gives an individual who wishes to view a particular movie available on videocassette who does not own or have the ability to rent a video cassette player the opportunity to view the cassette at the Nickelodeon. But for the Defendants' rental of the Nickelodeon viewing rooms, individuals who rent videocassettes would view them in a private place *i.e.*, the individual's home, rather than in a place open to the public such as Maxwell's or the Nickelodeon. It is this factor that distinguishes the Defendants' activities from simple rental of videocassettes to home users under the Copyright Act. As pointed out by the Plaintiffs, this difference is of considerable importance to

the copyright holders; ". . . A person's home is not rented out in two hour shifts to afford separate groups of persons the opportunity to see a variety of motion pictures. Nickelodeon's rooms are." . . . The operation of the Nickelodeon greatly increases the number of people able to view videocassettes of the Plaintiffs' copyrighted works.[5]

The case was determined in the plaintiffs' favor without oral argument. The appeal went to the Third Circuit Court of Appeals, the same court that heard the Redd Horne case, but to a different panel of judges. Much of the comment in the Appellate Court decision centered on the defendants' argument that the dispersed location of video-cassette players in the Nickelodeons was significantly different from the central placement of the machines at Maxwell's. The court rejected that argument and in so doing provided an added definition of public place:

> The Copyright Act speaks of performances at a place open to the public. It does not require that the public place be actually crowded with people. A telephone booth, a taxi cab, and even a pay toilet are commonly regarded as "open to the public," even though they are usually occupied only by one party at a time. Our opinion in *Redd Horne* turned not on the precise whereabouts of the video cassette players, but on the nature of Maxwell's stores. Maxwell's, like Aveco, was willing to make a viewing room and a video cassette available to any member of the public with the inclination to avail himself of this service. It is this availability that made Maxwell's stores public places, not the coincidence that the video cassette players were situated in the lobby. Because we find *Redd Horne* indistinguishable from the case at bar, we find that Aveco's operations constituted an authorization of public performances of Producers' copyrighted works.[6]

Thus, the district court decision was sustained. These two Appellate Court decisions suggest performances in almost any place open to the public, such as in libraries, museums, hospitals, churches, camps, prisons, etc. are subject to the copyright proprietors' control. The fact the performances are seen by only one person at a time does not appear to be relevant. Although the Redd Horne and Nickelodeon decisions could be modified or overturned, that seems unlikely. It seems safe to assume these two appellate court decisions have firmly defined the proprietors' right to regulate video performances in semi-public and public places in the foreseeable future.

The only realistic exemptions to the copyright proprietors' control are the home-use and business-meeting exemptions provided in Sect. 106, and the classroom use exemption provided in Sect. 110(1). These exemptions are discussed in the following chapters.

CHAPTER 2:

HOME-USE RIGHTS

There has been much discussion of "home-use rights" in video performances. That right appears in a curious fashion in Sect. 106, the section that grants proprietors the right to control performances.

Sect. 106. Exclusive rights in copyrighted works.

Subject to Sections 107 through 118, the owner of copyright under this title has the exclusive rights to do and to authorize any of the following:

. . .

(4) In the case of literary, musical, dramatic, and choreographic works, pantomimes, and motion pictures and other audiovisual works, to perform the copyrighted work publicly; . . .[1]

This gives proprietors substantial control over performances, but the control is limited by the last word, "publicly," which is defined as: "To perform or display it at a place open to the public or at any place where a substantial number of persons outside of a normal circle of a family and its social acquaintances is gathered;"[2] This provides two criteria for defining public performance: the performance must be open to the public *or* the performance must be open to a nonsubstantial number of persons outside of a normal circle of a family and its social acquaintances.

A home-use exemption, as such, is not included in the law. The term arose as a convenient definition of nonpublic performances held in the home. Clearly, this exemption authorizes performances in the home viewed by the family and its friends. The number of friends and family that may attend is unclear, and it will probably not be defined soon. On the other hand, the Redd Horne and Nickelodeon decisions state clearly that performances for single viewers that are sequentially accessible to the public, are public performances.

The issue of performances outside the home which are limited to a small number of people is more difficult to define. That topic is treated in Chapter 6.

CHAPTER 3:

EDUCATORS' RIGHTS

Educators' performance rights appear in Sect. 110, which includes ten exceptions to the proprietors' right to control performances and displays. Only one applies to performances of audiovisual works, and that appears in Sect. 110(1). That section authorizes almost all types of performances and displays in face-to-face teaching in non-profit educational institutions.

Sect. 110. Limitations on exclusive rights: Exemption of certain performances and displays.

Notwithstanding the provisions of section 106, the following are not infringements of copyright:

(1) performance or display of a work by instructors or pupils in the course of face-to-face teaching activities of a nonprofit educational institution, in a classroom or similar place devoted to instruction, unless, in the case of a motion picture or other audiovisual work, the performance, or the display of individual images, is given by means of a copy that was not lawfully made under this title, and that the person responsible for the performance knew or had reason to believe was not lawfully made; . . .[1]

The House or Representatives committee report that accompanied the copyright act defines several key phrases:

> The "teaching activities" exempted by the clause encompass systematic instruction of a very wide variety of subjects, but they do not include performances or displays, whatever their cultural value or intellectual appeal, that are given for recreation or entertainment of any part of their audience.[2]

> "[I]n the course of face-to-face teaching activities" is intended to exclude broadcasting or other transmissions from an outside location into classrooms, whether radio or television and whether open or closed circuit. However, as long as the instructor and pupils are in the same building or general area, the exemption would extend to the use of devices for amplifying or reproducing sounds and for projecting visual images.[3]

> Instructors or pupils — . . . the performance or display must be "by instructors or pupils," thus ruling out performances by actors, singers, or instrumentalists brought in from outside the school to put on a program. However, the term "instructors" would be broad enough to include guest lecturers if their instructional activities remain confined to classroom situations. In general, the term "pupils" refers to the enrolled members of a class.[4]

> Classroom or similar place. — the teaching activities exempted by the clause must take place "in a classroom or similar place devoted to instruction." For example, performances in an auditorium or stadium during a school assembly, graduation ceremony, class play, or sporting event, where the audience is not confined to the members of a particular class, would fall

outside the scope of clause (4) of section 110. The "similar place" referred to in clause (1) is a place which is "devoted to instruction" in the same way a classroom is; common examples would include a studio, a workshop, a gymnasium, a training field, a library, the stage of an auditorium, or the auditorium itself, if it is actually used as a classroom for systematic instructional activities.[5]

Further clarification appears in *The Supplementary Report of the Register of Copyrights on the General Revision of the U.S. Copyright Law: 1965 Bill:*

[T]hat the word "institution," while broad enough to cover a wide range of establishments engaging in teaching activities, is not intended to cover "organizations," "foundations," "associations," or similar "educational" groups not primarily and directly engaged in instruction.[6]

To summarize, Sect. 110(1) authorizes the performance and display of any copyrighted work in face-to-face teaching, but it imposes some limitations:

1. Performances and displays of audiovisual works must be made from legitimate copies, including prerecorded videocassettes;

2. Performances and displays must be part of a systematic course of instruction and not for the entertainment, recreation or cultural value of any part of the audience;

3. Performances and displays must be given by the instructors or pupils;

4. Performances and displays must be given in classrooms and other places devoted to instruction;

5. Performances and displays must be part of the teaching activities of nonprofit educational institutions; and

6. Attendance is limited to the instructors, pupils, and guest lecturers.

These six provisions are simple enough to be readily applied to nonprofit schools, colleges, and universities. In fact, the exemption is so broad that it seems unlikely it could be altered by anything short of an amendment to the copyright act. But the law is not always as simple as it appears, especially in the application of the sixth criterion, "nonprofit educational institution," which is not defined in the law. This issue does not appear to involve nonprofit public, private, and church-related schools and colleges, so it is postponed to Chapter 5.

EDUCATIONAL TRANSMISSIONS

Educators continue to raise questions about the legality of transmitting videocassettes to classes through closed-circuit transmission systems. The copyright proprietors insist that privilege is reserved to them in Sect. 110(2), but educators cite the same section of the law, plus other sources, to authorize closed-circuit instructional transmissions. The issue is confusing, but it can be resolved through a close reading of the law:

Sect. 110. Limitations on exclusive rights: Exemption of certain performances and displays

Notwithstanding the provisions of section 106, the following are not infringements of copyright:

. . .

(2) performance of a nondramatic literary or musical work or display of a work, by or in the course of a transmission, if—

(A) the performance or display is a regular part of the systematic instructional activities of a governmental body or a nonprofit educational institution; and

(B) the performance or display is directly related and of material assistance to the teaching content of the transmission; . . .[7]

At first glance, this appears to authorize instructional transmissions through open- and closed-circuit systems. The confusion arises from the definition of key words. Sect. 110(2) contains three key limitations in the phrases: nondramatic works, literary works, and musical works. Dramatic, nondramatic and musical, are not defined in the law, but they are clear enough without further definition. The restriction on performing videocassettes appears in the innocuous phrase, "literary work," which is defined in the law:

"Literary works" are works, other than audiovisual works, expressed in words, numbers, or other verbal or numerical symbols or indicia, regardless of the nature of the material objects, such as books, periodicals, manuscripts, phonorecords, films, tapes, disks, or cards, in which they are embodied.[8]

The limitation is in the first eight words: "literary works are works, other than audiovisual works . . ." Because of this clause, educational transmissions are limited to nondramatic literary or musical works—and audiovisual works are excluded by definition from this category.

Educators also cite the second sentence of the following quotation from the House report to authorize in-building and campus-wide instructional transmissions:

> "[I]n the course of face-to-face teaching activities" is intended to exclude broadcasting or other transmissions from an outside location into classrooms, whether radio or television and whether open or closed circuit. However, as long as the instructor and pupils are in the same building or general area, the exemption would extend to the use of devices for amplifying or reproducing sounds and for projecting visual images.[9]

Some interpret the second sentence as a modification of the restriction on video transmissions in Sect. 110(2). No one seems to know what the committee intended when it wrote that sentence; its greatest apparent value is to help justify the use of public address systems and remote control projectors in lecture halls. Whatever its purpose, this interesting piece of legislative history does not supersede the law, so copyrighted programs cannot be transmitted through closed-circuit transmission systems without a license. Although these transmission rights are reserved, many educational film and video distributors grant closed-circuit, educational transmission licenses free upon request. Other firms charge a small fee for transmission licenses.

BENEFIT PERFORMANCES

Educators sometimes suggest that the benefit performance exemption in Sect. 110(4) authorizes some video performances. A quick reading of the law, suggests that in terpretation, but as in the preceding paragraph, the definition of "literary work," blocks that interpretation. The act states:

> Sect. 110. Limitations on exclusive rights: Exemptions of certain performances and displays.

> Notwithstanding the provisions of section 106, the following are not infringements of copyright:

> . . .

> > (4) performance of a nondramatic literary or musical work otherwise than in a transmission to the public, without any purpose of direct or indirect commercial advantage and without payment of any fee or other compensation for the performance to any of its performances, promoters, or organizers, if—

> > > (A) there is no direct or indirect admission charge; or

> > > (B) the proceeds, after deducting the reasonable costs of producing the performance, are used exclusively for educational, religious, or charitable purposes and not for private financial gain. . . .[10]

This is the legal basis for most free performances, such as storytelling in libraries and performances by school bands and glee clubs. However, as in the preceding paragraph, the definition of "literary work," prevents any type of video performance, regardless of its instructional or cultural value.

PERFORMANCES IN RESIDENCE-HALL LOUNGES

The 1987 annual conference of the Association of College and University Residence Hall Officers International included two programs on copyright restrictions on video performances in residence hall lounges. It was reported there that several universities have received cease-and-desist letters as a result of residence hall video performances. Some universities (e.g., the University of Southern California) responded by terminating all video performances in residence hall lounges. Many universities acquire annual nontheatrical public performance licenses authorizing performances in residence hall lounges.

The question arises about residence halls being the students' home and the application of the home-use exemption to residence halls. Students who have videodisc or videocassette recorders in their private rooms are entitled to the home-use exemption discussed in Chapter 2. On the other hand, there is little question that performances in residence halls that are accessible to non-residents or a large number of residents are public performances and require a license. Two firms, Films Inc. and Swank Audio-Visuals, sell a variety of licenses in this market and there seems to be no justification for continuing unlicensed video performances accessible to non-residents or a large number of residents.

The difficult question centers on video performances in small lounges accessible to a limited number of students. Many of these lounges are locked and only a few students living in adjacent rooms have keys to them. Residence hall administrators argue that recent court cases affecting residence hall privacy make these small lounges part of the students' private quarters. The law seems unclear on this point. Some administrators have developed a two-step *modus vivendi* awaiting clarification of the issue. They buy licenses for video performances in large lounges but permit unlicensed video performances in small lounges, if attendance in the small lounges is restricted to a few residents who have a key to the lounge.

In conclusion, the Copyright Act, whether intentionally or accidentally, prohibits performances of audiovisual works, including videocassettes, except under the educational exemption, the home-use exemption, the business meeting exemption, or with a license.

USING COPYRIGHTED VIDEOCASSETTES

CHAPTER 4:

LIBRARIANS' RIGHTS

When the copyright revision bill was being written, librarians lobbied effectively to receive a generous exemption for photocopying machines, but they did not request a performance exemption for libraries. A leader of the library lobby during that period indicated they did not anticipate a problem with audiovisual performances in libraries, so they did not request an exemption for in-library performances. Until recently, most librarians were unaware of the performance limitations on in-house showings and the copyright proprietors showed little interest in marketing licenses to libraries. The matter might have remained that way were it not for the decisions in the Redd Horne and Nickelodeon cases that narrowly defined performance rights. Since libraries did not receive a performance exemption in the copyright revision act and the courts have held to a narrow definition of public performances, video performances in libraries must take place under the teaching exemption, the business-meeting exemption, or with a license.

THE TEACHING EXEMPTION

The teaching exemption has obvious applications for school libraries or learning resource centers (hereafter libraries). Modern educational theories suggest classes should be divided periodically to provide specialized instruction for pupils. Classes are frequently divided so pupils who are having difficulty with a lesson can review the material while their classmates study enrichment material. Practical considerations frequently prompt teachers to send part of a class to the library for individual-or group-instruction by the librarian or media specialist (hereafter librarian) while the rest of the class remains with the teacher. As a consequence of these and other responsibilities, school librarians are certified professional educators and serve as part of the teaching team. A school librarian who teaches a class or assists a student with a lesson functions as a teacher. As such, he or she may perform relevant copyrighted works to support the lesson. When students are sent to the library for make-up work, enrichment learning, or research, they are working under the teacher's or librarian's direction, so performances given under these circumstances also appear to meet the above requirements.

When applying Sect. 110(1) to instruction in libraries, the question frequently centers on the "place" requirement—the performance must take place "in a classroom or similar place devoted to instruction. . . ."[1] The house report provides a specific definition of "similar place":

> The "similar place" referred to in clause (1) is a place which is "devoted to instruction" in the same way a classroom is; common examples would include a studio, a workshop, a gymnasium, a training field, a library, the stage of an auditorium, or the auditorium itself, if it is actually used as a classroom for systematic instructional activities.[2]

It appears then that individual or group instruction in

the library of a nonprofit school, college, or university meets the "place" requirement. But "place" is not the only requirement—as each performance also must meet the remaining conditions of Sect. 110(1), which are summarized in the preceding chapter.

One question remains about video performances in school and college libraries. Some videocassettes purchased for class use, especially films purchased for film-study classes, attract students who want to view them for recreational purposes. Since these materials cannot be performed for recreational purposes under Sect. 110(1), such performances are probably infringements which should be discouraged, unless the performances are given under a license.

PUBLIC LIBRARY PERFORMANCES

When school, college, or university classes meet in public libraries, there is little doubt that the Sect. 110(1) exemption applies to those courses, so long as all the requirements are met. But public libraries frequently sponsor lectures and workshops to meet local demands. Libraries operate at a disadvantage in applying the Sect. 110(1) exemption to these situations. If a public library is sued for performing videocassettes in lectures or workshops it sponsors, it may have to prove:

1. It is a "nonprofit educational institution,"

2. The course meets the "systematic course of instruction," test, and

3. The library meets the other requirements of Sect. 110(1).

A lawsuit focusing on this issue could be long and expensive and the outcome is not assured. A public library would appear to be at a significant disadvantage if the performances were accessible to persons other than enrolled students. Performances of videocassettes during lectures and workshops sponsored by public libraries may be legitimate performances under Sect. 110(1), but librarians should be especially careful to meet all the requirements of Sect. 110(1).

DOES THE HOME-USE EXEMPTION APPLY TO LIBRARIES?

Librarians frequently suggest that individuals who are too poor to own their own videocassette recorders can use library equipment to watch videocassettes. This appealing argument suggests that performances in viewing rooms or carrels occupied by one person, a family, or a small group of friends, meets the private showing requirement for the home use exemption. Although that argument seems persuasive, it does not reflect the decision in the Redd Horne and Nickelodeon cases described in Chapter 1. In the Redd Horne case, Maxwell's video stores were equipped with small viewing rooms, with seating for two to four persons and a color television receiver. Viewers chose a film, paid a rental fee, and saw the film on the television receiver. The videocassette playback machines were operated by an employee.[3] The facts in the Nickelodeon case were almost identical except that each booth had its own videocassette playback machine which was operated by the client.[4] The plaintiffs charged the performances in these two cases infringed their copyrights, as defined in Sects. 101 and 106. The defendants employed several avenues of defense, but the defense under copyright was based on the fact the occupants of each viewing room were single individuals, friends, or members of a family, so the showings were exempt private showings as defined in Sects. 101 and 106. The court found that since the performances were accessible *ad seriatim* to the general public, they were not exempt private showings.

DO THE REDD HORNE AND NICKELODEON DECISIONS APPLY TO LIBRARIES?

Public libraries sometimes respond that Maxwell's and Nickelodeon charged an admission fee to see the performances and libraries provide video performances free of charge. The decisions in these two cases did not focus on *charges* for performances but on the *availability* of the performances to the general public. On the basis of these two decisions, there seems little doubt that public performances of copyrighted videocassettes in public library viewing rooms and carrels are sequentially accessible to the general public. Performances given in these circumstances, without a license, infringe the proprietors' performance rights. Charging for the performance may only add an additional evidence of the seriousness of the infringement. Librarians sometimes argue that private viewing rooms and video carrels in libraries are restricted areas and not public places. This is a convenient argument, but it clearly contradicts the appellate court's definition of public places in Nickelodeon:

> The Copyright Act speaks of performances at a place open to the public. It does not require that the public place be actually crowded with people. A telephone booth, a taxi cab, and even a pay toilet are commonly regarded as "open to the public," even though they are usually occupied only by one party at a time. [5]

Some argue that Maxwell's and Nickelodeon were commercial firms, so those decisions do not apply to nonprofit libraries. None of the district and appellate court decisions mentioned profiting from the performances, so that is a doubtful argument.

The court seems determined to establish a narrow definition of "public place." A library video carrel seems no less public than a telephone booth, a taxi cab, or a pay toilet, so it is time for librarians to reassess video performances in libraries. Several public libraries have received cease-and-desist letters from Sargoy Stein & Hanft (the firm representing the plaintiffs in Redd Horne and Nickelodeon) and from other firms in an effort to stop unauthorized library performances. Librarians must recognize that video performances for patrons in public libraries, except classroom performances authorized under Sect. 110(1), are copyright infringements. It is time for librarians to take appropriate steps to conform to the law.

TWO ALTERNATE VIEWS

The major film companies suffered one defeat in their effort to narrow the definition of public performances. In *Columbia Pictures* v. *Professional Real Estate Investors*, several MPAA member firms sued the La Mancha Private Club and Villas, an exclusive Palm Springs hotel. Each hotel suite was equipped with a video disc player and color receiver and guests could rent videodiscs from the hotel gift shop. The lower court determined that the decisions in Redd Horne and Nickelodeon did not apply because a hotel room is a private facility which serves as a short-term private dwelling. The court cited the Fourth Amendment and several cases to support the right of privacy when occupying a hotel room. It commented:

> In this respect, hotel rooms are not different from private homes. Similarly, viewing movies in a hotel

– 26 –

room would be an incidental form of entertainment, and is no different from viewing movies in a home. Home use of videos is admittedly a private and not a public performance.

> For these reasons, a hotel room is not a place open to the public under the copyright laws and the viewing of video movies in such accommodations is not a public performance under the copyright laws. . . .[6]

The argument has been made that the decision in this case shelters private performances in public libraries.[7] The above quotation indicates the case hinges on a substantial body of statutory and case law protecting privacy in hotel rooms as an extension of the home. This decision has no visible application to video performances in libraries.

A more frequently expressed view appears in "Library and Classroom Use of Copyrighted Videotapes and Computer Software," by Mary Hutchings Reed and Debra Stanek, which was distributed by the American Library Association. It states, in part:

I. Videotapes

B. In-library Use in Public Libraries

> 1. Most performances of a videotape in a public room as part of an entertainment or cultural program, whether a fee is charged or not, would be infringing and a performance license is required from the copyright owner.

> 2. To the extent a videotape is used in an educational program conducted in a library's public room, the performance will not be in-

fringing if the requirements for classroom use are met. . . .

3. Libraries which allow groups to use or rent their public meeting rooms should, as part of their rental agreement, require the group to warrant that it will secure all necessary performance licenses and indemnify the library for any failure on their part to do so.

4. If patrons are allowed to view videotapes on library-owned equipment, they should be limited to private performances, i.e. one person, or no more than one family, at a time.

5. User charges for private viewings should be nominal and directly related to the cost of maintenance of the videotape.

6. Even if a videotape is labelled "For Home Use Only," private viewings in the library should be considered to be authorized by the vendor's sale to the library with imputed knowledge of the library's intended use of the videotape.

7. Notices may be posted on videorecorders or players used in the library to educate and warn patrons about the existence of the copyright laws, such as: MANY VIDEO-TAPED MATERIALS ARE PROTECTED BY COPYRIGHT. 17 U.S.C. SECT 101. UNAUTHORIZED COPYING MAY BE PROHIBITED BY LAW. (Emphasis in original)[8]

This seven-point statement expresses the views of many librarians, but it appears to contain two significant errors. Item 4 indicates private performances for individuals and families are not public performances and do not require a performance license. That fails to reflect the Redd Horne and Nickelodeon decisions, which categorically state that performances to individuals and small groups, which are serially accessible to the general public, are public performances.

An additional error appears in item 6. Hutchings Reed and Stanek make the common mistake of assuming that vendors of videocassettes are the copyright proprietors. Copyrights in videocassettes are usually owned by the producers, but sales in ancillary markets (which includes libraries) are normally handled by independent distributors who have little or no control over the copyrights. A sale by an independent distributor to a library cannot automatically incur a commitment if the distributor does not control the performance rights to the work. One should never assume the acquisition of performance rights with the purchase or lease of a film or videocassette, unless the performance right is specifically granted.

The above position is closely related to one taken by Stanek in *Information Technology and Libraries*, which was written under the direction of Mary Hutchings Reed.[9] Stanek states that large public showings, other than classroom showings authorized by Sect. 110(1), are infringements. She goes on to say:

> What about libraries that permit individuals or small groups of persons to watch videotapes in private viewing rooms: Such performances are public performances, but they may be a fair use of the materials and therefore not infringing.

In the case of a videotape, showing its images in any sequence or making its accompanying sounds audible constitutes a performance. Under the Section 101 definition of *publicly*, even performances in a private room in a library could be public because a library is a place open to the public. Therefore, such performances are infringing unless they can be said to be fair uses of the copyrighted work (17 U.S.C. Sect. 107).[10]

The article then gives a step-by-step application of the four fair use criteria to performances in private viewing rooms. The potential error here is that the fair use section of the law, as presently defined, pertains to "reproduction in copies," and not to performance rights. William F. Patry's *The Fair Use Privilege in Copyright Law* is the leading scholarly book on fair use, and it makes no references to the application of the fair use concept to performances.[11] Stanek offers a novel interpretation of fair use, but fails to cite a single court decision or authoritative work to sustain her position. Novel theories are the sign of commendable intellectual endeavor, but legal theories that directly contradict recently established legal precedent are probably unreliable. In brief, Stanek's theory seems doomed in the light of the narrow definition of "public performance" in the Redd Horne and Nickelodeon decisions. It seems unwise for libraries to base decisions about public performance rights on this speculative article which substantially contradicts recent case law.

This interpretation is renewed in *The Copyright Primer for Librarians and Educators*, by Mary Hutchings Reed. The author states that large group showings require a license, but suggests:

> If patrons are allowed to view videotapes on library-owned equipment, they should be limited to

private performances, i.e., one person or no more than a small number of persons or a family and its social acquaintances, at one time.[12]

Again, we must return to the recent court decisions in Redd Horne and Nickelodeon. The court states firmly that performances to one person or a small number of persons which is sequentially available to the public are public performances which require a license. The two court decisions did not offer any exceptions or suggest any variances in its decision, so it seems unwise to perpetuate such a nebulous hope of an exemption for library video performances.

The film and video industry is disturbed about Hutchings Reed's position. Since she is ALA's attorney, industry representatives view her published and oral statements as the official position of the American Library Association. This concern led to an exchange of letters between Harvey Shapiro, an attorney with Sargoy, Stein & Hanft, who represents MPAA, and Thomas J. Galvin, Executive Director of ALA. Shapiro restated the industry interpretation of the proprietors' rights and Galvin restated Hutchings Reed's position. The issue was far from resolution, so Charles Benton, President of PMI/Films, Inc., arranged for a face-to-face discussion of the issue, on July 6, 1987.[13] At the meeting, the ALA representatives distributed copies of Hutchings Reed's new book, *The Copyright Primer for Librarians and Educators*. After that, each side restated its position. The only agreement was to meet again to develop guidelines. The two parties are far from agreement, so it may take a long time to prepare guidelines. Industry representatives indicate that libraries will continue to receive cease-and-desist letters, on a case-by-case basis, for unauthorized public performances. Industry representatives also indicate they will not make a concentrated effort to enforce their performance rights in libraries while the discussions continue.

IF WE CAN SHOW FILMS, WHY CAN'T WE SHOW VIDEO?

Libraries have conducted film showings for over fifty years without question of copyright infringement, so it is not unreasonable that librarians should question this restriction on video performances. The change is a result of the Copyright Revision Act of 1976. Under the 1909 law, when the proprietors sold one print of a film, they lost the right to regulate performances of that title. To maintain control over performances, the studios stopped selling theatrical films, and began distributing them through licensing agreements. Nontheatrical films were sold to schools, colleges, and libraries under life-of-the-print contracts which limited exhibitions to free performances by nonprofit agencies. (Contracts are treated at greater length in Chapter 7.) The new copyright act completely revised performance rights and gave copyright proprietors comprehensive control over performances of their films, but most educational film distributors retained the established system for distributing nontheatrical 16mm films. While the old distribution procedures may have been retained for 16mm films, videocassettes represent a new venture and the distributors have chosen to conduct that business under the more favorable rules of the new copyright act.

POTENTIAL EXCEPTIONS

Several exceptions to the restrictions on in-library video performances seem obvious. Many non-theatrical videocassettes are cleared for in-library performances. Information about performance rights is not always readily available, but inquiries with the distributor will reveal this information. It would be helpful if all library reviewing sources would follow the example of *The Video Librarian*, which identifies the performance rights for each title it reviews.[14]

Patrons sometimes ask for help in operating new or borrowed video equipment. A quick demonstration is infinitely more helpful than words and gestures, so it seem reasonable to demonstrate equipment operation on a library machine. If the patron sees a few moments of a program during this demonstration, one might argue that it was an infringing performance. However, *de minimis non curat lex* ("The law does not care for, or take notice of, very small or trifling matters") [15] would appear to offer ample defense for an incidental viewing of a few moments of a program while learning to use the machine.

Furthermore, librarians must evaluate videocassettes for purchase, rental, or removal from the collection. As long as individual or small-group performances are solely for professional evaluation and are not accessible to the public, they do not appear to be public performances and may fall under the business-meeting exemption discussed in Chapter 6. Similarly, librarians may need to view a video program to catalog it or respond to clients' complaints. These also may be acceptable performances under the above exemption. Finally, performances as a part of staff training may fit in the business-meeting exemption. Librarians should apply this exemption carefully and should not attempt to stretch the business-meeting exemption to cover public performances.

POTENTIAL SOLUTIONS

The Redd Horne and Nickelodeon decisions clearly sustain the proprietors' claim to control public performances of videocassettes, including performances in carrels and private viewing rooms. As a result, the law does not appear to authorize public performances of videocassettes in libraries, except under the face-to-face teaching exemption. This creates serious problems for pubic libraries that invested in video equipment for patron use within the library. Several solutions may be considered:

1. Stop all library video performances,

2. Continue present practices and hope for the best,

3. Limit showings to educational and inspirational works which can be performed without a license,

4. Obtain blanket clearances,

5. Obtain performance licenses, or

6. Amend the law to authorize free performances of copyrighted films and videocassettes in nonprofit libraries.

The first alternative, terminating in-house performances, is unimaginative and should be discouraged. The second approach, maintaining status quo, is not recommended, though it appears to be the policy in most public libraries. The third alternative, using titles cleared for showing in the library, is safe, but it denies access to hundreds of desirable titles.

The fourth alternative, obtaining blanket clearances, is used by at least one large public library. It involves sending video distributors a form letter advising that the library is uncertain whether it can legally show videocassettes in carrels, viewing rooms, and auditoriums. To avoid potential infringements, the library has adopted a policy limiting videocassette purchases to vendors who give the library written permission for free performances. (A sample letter appears in Appendix A.) Copyright proprietors have a longstanding and justifiable aversion to indefinite, blanket permissions, so most distributors will forgo library orders before granting limited or indefinite blanket permissions. Furthermore, most distributors handle titles under fixed-duration licenses (some as short as six months) and they cannot make legal commitments beyond the expiration date of the license. Libraries would probably achieve better cooperation from vendors by only requesting clearance for two to four years.

The fifth alternative, obtaining video licenses, is new to libraries, but the procedure is simple. MGM/UA sold its first public library video performance license to the Los Angeles County Public Library in 1983. MGM/UA licenses are now handled by an independent distributor, who has been joined by other firms that offer performance licenses. Several public libraries and library systems are now acquiring licenses for in-house performances. An alternative may be available through blanket performance licenses offered by several firms. Licenses are discussed at greater length in Chapter 7.

The last alternative, amending the copyright law, could be difficult, especially in the light of the Congressional reluctance to handle additional copyright legislation. If an amendment were deemed to be the best solution, it should consist of a new subsection to Section 110. The amendment might read:

Sect. 110. Limitations on exclusive rights: Exemption of certain performances and displays

Notwithstanding the provisions of section 106, the following are not infringements of copyright:

. . .

(11) performances and displays of motion pictures

and other audiovisual works in non-profit libraries and archives qualifying under Title 17, *United States Code*, Section 108(a)(2), if:

(a) the performances and displays are open to the public at large;

(b) there is no direct or indirect admission charge; and

(c) The performances are without any purpose of direct or indirect commercial advantage.

Title 17, *U.S.C*, Section 108(a)(2) identifies libraries and archives qualifying for the library photocopying privileges. The library community may not be able to get this amendment passed, but if it mounts a serious effort, the film industry may reassess performances in libraries, and offer more attractive licenses.

CAN LIBRARIES LOAN VIDEOCASSETTES FOR HOME USE?

With the concern about infringing performances and the sale of performance licenses, readers may wonder if libraries can circulate videocassettes for home use. Fortunately, they can. Sect. 109(a) incorporates the "first sale doctrine," which limits a proprietor's control over a work after it is published or enters commercial distribution:

Notwithstanding the provisions of section 106(3), the owner of a particular copy or phonorecord lawfully made under this title, or any person authorized by such owner, is entitled, without the authority of the copyright owner, to sell or otherwise dispose of the possession of that copy or phonorecord.[16]

That muddy legal prose is translated in the house report:

> Section 109(a) restates and confirms the principle that, where the copyright owner has transferred ownership of a particular copy or phonorecord of a work, the person to whom the copy or phonorecord is transferred is entitled to dispose of it by sale, rental, or any other means. . . . A library that has acquired ownership of a copy is entitled to lend it under any conditions it chooses to impose. . . .[17]

This basic right appeared in the 1909 and 1976 copyright acts but was amended in 1984 to authorize a surcharge on commercial rentals of sound recordings. Rentals of sound recordings by nonprofit libraries were specifically excluded from this amendment.[18]

USING COPYRIGHTED VIDEOCASSETTES

CHAPTER 5:
HOSPITAL, CHURCH AND INDUSTRIAL TRAINING SPECIALISTS' RIGHTS

Hospital, church, and industrial training specialists encounter many problems in determining their right to perform videocassettes in their workplace. Some video performances in these environments are exempt under Sect. 110(1), but most performances fall into a large grey area that has not been adequately addressed. Comprehensive guidance cannot be supplied for many situations, but this chapter attempts to place the issues in perspective in the hope that better answers will be available soon.

PERFORMANCES IN HOSPITALS:

Video performances in hospitals fall into several categories: college and university classes, staff training, public service health education, and patient entertainment. Each of these performances involves a different aspect of the copyright law, so they must be treated separately.

College and university classes:

Video performances in classes taught in hospitals by colleges and universities which are part of an ongoing college or university instructional program are exempt under Sect. 110(1) if the appropriate conditions are met. This issue is treated at length in Chapters 3 and 4 and will not be repeated here, but it should be noted that the "place" requirement in Sect. 110(1) can be met if the class meets in a hospital classroom, meeting room, laboratory, theater, or other facility that separates the teacher and pupils from persons who are not enrolled in the class. Regularly scheduled classes conducted in for-profit hospitals by non-profit colleges and universities appear to qualify, as the exemption is essentially tied to the nonprofit character of the teaching institution and not to the place where classes are held.

Private staff showings:

Performances in meetings and staff training programs which are not exempt under Sect. 110(1) may be exempt under a little-studied aspect of Sect. 106(4). The definition of "publicly" in Sect. 101, when applied to Section 106(4), appears to authorize non-public performances in government offices and places of business. The exemption, usually called the business-meeting exemption, is not very explicit, but it appears to authorize private staff performances:

To perform or display a work "publicly" means —

(1) to perform or display it at a place open to the public or at any place where a substantial number of persons outside of a normal circle of a family and its social acquaintances is gathered. . . .[1]

— 40 —

The key phrase is "or at any place where a substantial number of persons outside of a normal circle of a family and its social acquaintances is gathered. . . ." The house report comments: "Routine meetings of business and governmental personnel would be excluded because they do not represent the gathering of a substantial number of persons."[2] Two conditions are required. The performance must not be accessible to anyone other than employees, and the performance must be limited to a nonsubstantial number of people. Substantial and nonsubstantial are not defined in the copyright act, so common sense must be applied here. The exemption appears to apply equally to performances in for-profit and non-profit hospitals and appears to include a variety of staff meetings and staff-training programs. This issue is treated at greater length in Chapter 6.

Public-service, health-education programs:

Many hospitals offer public service health education programs for expectant parents, and for persons suffering from various diseases. These programs do not lead to an accredited degree or certificate, but are part of a public service effort. Video performance in these classes may not qualify for the Sect. 110(1) exemption because the hospital may not meet the "nonprofit educational institution" test and, more importantly, the course may not meet the "systematic course of instruction" test. The following quotation from a 1965 Copyright Office report is illustrative of the nonprofit educational institution test:

[T]hat the word "institution," while broad enough to cover a wide range of establishments engaging in teaching activities, is not intended to cover "organizations," "foundations," "associations," or similar "educational" groups not primarily and directly engaged in instruction.[3]

The last seven words "not primarily and directly engaged in instruction" seem particularly significant. Hospitals are generally viewed as places of healing and not as educational institutions. It remains to be seen if the courts will accept health education programs offered by hospitals as evidence of the hospital's role as an educational institution.

The "systematic course of instruction" test also must be considered if hospitals are to qualify for the Sect. 110(1) exemption. Many health education programs do not include the usual apparatus of school or college courses, such as demanding examinations, written reports, and the like. Students in these classes usually do not receive grades. In most instances it might be difficult to prove these programs meet the systematic-course-of-instruction test.

This issue has not been addressed by the courts and clearcut answers cannot be supplied until precedent is established in this or a similar situation. Those who teach or support hospital public-service, health-education programs should proceed carefully. Video programs designed specifically for these courses may be sold with suitable performance rights. If not, the rights may be available free, on request, or they may be sold for a nominal sum. It would be unwise, though, to assume those rights are always present or are unnecessary.

Patient entertainment:

Video performances offered for the entertainment of patients in hospitals are not exempt performances, regardless of their humanitarian, educational, cultural, or counseling value. These are public performances, as defined in the Redd Horne and Nickelodeon cases, and performance licenses are required. In 1985 the Veterans Administration acquired licenses from MGM/UA for videocassette performances in all VA hospitals. Other hospitals and hospital chains later purchased performance licenses from MGM/UA. Recently, a few hospitals have purchased performance licenses from the Motion Picture Licensing Corp.

In May of 1987, Rep. Dan Glickman, of Kansas, introduced an amendment to the copyright act titled, the "Patients' Viewing Rights Act."[4] The bill would authorize most video performances in hospitals on condition that the videocassette recorder was not supplied by the hospital. This bill has an interesting history. Mr. Glickman introduced the bill in response to a complaint from constituents that a local nonprofit organization, was unable to secure reasonably-priced performance licenses to show videocassettes to children hospitalized for cancer treatment. The organization is Parents Against Leukemia and Malignancy Society (P.A.L.M.S.). The society is a local organization of parents of children who are receiving cancer treatment at St. Francis Hospital, in Wichita. For many years, P.A.L.M.S. owned projectors and purchased films to show to the children in the pediatric ward. It later used memorial funds to purchase two videocassette recorders to show videocassettes to hospitalized children. (The videocassettes are loaned free of charge by a Wichita store.) The hospital administration became concerned about copyright infringements in these performances and required P.A.L.M.S. to secure performance license for the showings. P.A.L.M.S. attempted to buy licenses from some of the studios and was referred to Films, Inc., which handles nontheatrical public performance licenses for several major studios. Films, Inc. offered a a one-year nontheatrical public performance license for $3,000. P.A.L.M.S. could not afford the fee and several of the leaders were angered by the responses they received from the studios and Films, Inc. Some of the parents appealed to Congressman Glickman for assistance. The congressman asked the Copyright Office for advice, and it suggested that he write to each studio that belongs to the Motion Picture Association of America (MPAA) and request a waiver of the performance fee for this humanitarian service. The studios did not grant the request, but Films, Inc. responded by selling P.A.L.M.S. a one-year license for titles produced by Paramount, Orion, Tri Star, 20th Century Fox, and MGM/UA. (Films, Inc. is not an MPAA member, but represents the above-mentioned MPAA members.) The license was issued in November 30, 1986 for $400. A Films, Inc. representative explained that the difference between the $3,000 and $400 licensing fees represents difference between a hospital-wide license for the 886 bed hospital ($3.39 per bed) and a license restricted to the 42 bed pediatric ward ($9.52 per bed). Films, Inc. says the $400 fee only covers the cost of record keeping, which is probably true. (P.A.L.M.S files monthly reports of performance given under the contract; Films, Inc. then reports the performances to the appropriate studios.)

Six months after P.A.L.M.S purchased the license from Films, Inc. Congressman Glickman introduced the "Patients' Viewing Rights Act." (The bill appears in Appendix E). After the bill was introduced, P.A.L.M.S. officials indicate the Walt Disney organization donated six videocassettes with performance rights and Warner Brothers sold it a one-year performance license for one dollar.[5] If the bill is enacted, it will permit performances and transmission for inpatients in health care facilities if the videocassette or videodisc player was provided by someone other than the hospital. (The television receiver could be provided by the hospital.) The film industry is concerned about this bill, as it represents an important exemption to their right to control performances. P.A.L.M.S members hope Congress will hold a hearing on the bill in the fall of 1987, but it had not been scheduled at the time of writing.

A related issue concerns performance for patients in nursing homes. The argument is made that most nursing home patients reside there permanently, so it becomes their residence. A video performance in the patient's room, in the presence of friends and relatives, undoubtedly constitutes a private performance in the patient's home. However, video performances in nursing homes are usually given in a common room, for any patient or visitor who cares to watch. Some attorneys argue persuasively that these rooms are open to the public as surely as the pay phones, taxicabs, and pay toilets cited in the Nickelodeon decision.[6]

A few years ago, a vice president of a major studio stated that video performances in common rooms of nursing homes were infringements, but his firm was not prepared, at that time, to prosecute those infringements. Industry leaders are loosing money from unlicensed performances in nursing homes, but they seem reluctant to sue. If the Glickman amendment passes, it may exempt performances in nursing homes. If it fails, some firms may be willing to sue nursing homes for unlicensed performances in common rooms and unlicensed transmissions to patients' rooms.

PERFORMANCES IN CHURCHES AND CHURCH MEETING ROOMS

Video performances in churches which are open to the congregation or to the public require a "nontheatrical public performance license." Inspirational programs available from church video distributors are frequently sold with suitable performance rights. On the other hand, videocassettes of feature films, television documentaries, and cartoon programs are rarely distributed with performance rights. The performance rights may be available from the producer or a licensing agency, but the distributors frequently do not control the performance rights to the products they sell. In short, do not assume the performance rights were acquired with the purchase, lease, or rental of videocassettes for church use.

Unlike performances held in churches, some video performances in church meeting rooms may be exempt. Programs shown there are offered for a variety of reasons. Some are continuing education programs offered for academic credit while others are designed to entertain the audience.

Continuing education courses are sometimes held in church meeting rooms for pastors and church workers. If attendance is limited to the instructor and students, and the course leads to a recognized degree, certificate, or ordination, the performances may be authorized under Sect. 110(1). One should verify that video performances given in these classes meet all the conditions discussed in Chapter 3.

On the other hand, church nursery programs frequently entertain children with video cartoons and other programs. Carefully chosen programs may have some training value, but these programs are obviously designed to entertain the children. Inasmuch as these programs appear to be accessible to the general public of the appropriate age, licenses are required.

Church-sponsored youth groups frequently show videocassettes at their meetings. Although every program may have some educational or moral value, most programs are designed to entertain the audience. Licenses are required for these performances. Some pastors hold youth meetings in their homes so the performances fall under the home-use exemption. Most copyright proprietors acknowledge that licenses are not required for video performances in the pastor's or church worker's home, attended by the family and friends. (See Chapter 2 for additional information about video performances in homes.)

Many other meetings and social gatherings are held on church property. These may be meetings organized by the church or they may be organized by outside groups. Examples include weekend retreats, summer camps, prayer meetings, or meetings held by outside groups, such as the Lions Club or Alcoholics Anonymous. In each instance, a license is required for video performances.

Church teachers frequently show videocassettes during sabbath, summer, after-school, and evening educational programs. Some of these programs are isolated and unrelated events which are not part of a systematic course of instruction. Others appear to be part of a regularly scheduled course of study. If these courses meet the systematic-course-of-instruction test, outlined in Chapters 3, the Sect. 110(1) exemption may apply to video performances in these classes. The law and legislative history are unclear on whether the classroom exemption was intended to cover church classes. This issue receives further treatment in the following section.

PROBLEM COURSES IN CHURCHES AND HOSPITALS

The key issues in applying the Sect. 110(1) exemption to church and hospital classes are: A. the nonprofit-educational-institution test and B. the systematic-course-of-instruction test. Many questions remain about some applications of the phrase, "nonprofit educational institution," in Section 110(l). The phrase is not defined in the law, but the House Report explains:

> Nonprofit educational institution. – Clause (l) makes clear that it applies only to the teaching activities "of a nonprofit educational institution," thus excluding from the exemption performances or displays in profit-making institutions such as dance studios, and language schools.[7]

To judge from the language of the law and the legislative history, it clearly authorizes performances in face-to-face teaching conducted by nonprofit schools, colleges, and universities, but other applications remain unclear. The phrase also may authorize performances of videocassettes in classes offered by other nonprofit agencies, including public-service, health-education courses offered by hospitals and religion courses offered by churches. This issue will probably have to be resolved by the courts.

Aside from the nonprofit aspect described above, the phrase "educational institution" is not defined by the copyright act or its legislative history. It also does not appear to have been tested in copyright court cases, but that and similar phrases have been applied in other cases. Some decisions appear to support the application of the Section 110(l) exemption to nonprofit institutions other than schools and colleges:

> School for continuing education of businessmen was "educational institution" within meaning of Real Property Tax Law exemption.[8]

> A free public library is an "educational institution."[9]

Nonprofit membership corporation which planned to conduct art classes for town residents and students in buildings on college campus, qualified as an "educational institution" within ordinance permitting educational institutions in a residential area when authorized by board of trustees of village, as corporation's objective had some educational value, it performed an educational function and it was organized exclusively for that purpose.[10]

But on the other hand:

Taxpayer, which espoused philosophy of cooperative education based on folkschool movement, which ran youth camps, a camp for families, one or two workshops and maintained a library containing 2,000 to 3,000 volumes, but which was not accredited, did not confer any degrees and offered no credits, was not an "educational institution" as such term was used in tax exemption statute.[11]

Ordinary meaning of "educational institution" which is exempt from inheritance taxes is a place where classes are conducted, such as schools and colleges, and not an institution which furnishes some education, no matter what branch, as incidental adjunct to its main purpose.[12]

Since "educational institution" does not appear to have achieved a uniform definition in the courts, another phrase in the house report deserves closer scrutiny. "Systematic instructional activities," is defined in the house report in its description of exempt performances in educational broadcasting:

The concept of "systematic instructional activities"

is intended as the general equivalent of "curriculums" but it could be broader in a case such as that of an institution using systematic teaching methods not related to specific course work.[13]

That is not the clearest definition in legislative history, but it suggests a broad application to performance rights authorized in Sect. 110(1). The Register of Copyright's 1965 report to the House Subcommittee on the Judiciary comments:

[T]he word "institution," while broad enough to cover a wide range of establishments engaging in teaching activities, is not intended to cover "organizations," "foundations," "associations," or similar "educational" groups not primarily and directly engaged in instruction.[14]

Melville B. Nimmer commented, "The exemption is probably applicable to private, non-proprietary educational institutions even if tuition or other fees are charged for the purpose of meeting operating expenses."[15]

The Sect. 110(1) exemption probably does not apply to every training program offered by churches, hospitals, and similar organizations. If a church or nonprofit hospital is sued for copyright infringement for unlicensed video performances, agencies with highly structured training programs which lead to degrees or certificates may be in an excellent position to defend themselves. On the other hand, agencies that offer occasional, casually-structured classes or retreats may have great difficulty defending video performances as an extension of Sect. 110(1).

Since the law and legislative history are not very helpful in defining the limits of the Sect. 110(1) exemption, it may be useful to offer a *preliminary* checklist for those attempting to apply the exemption to their educational programs:

1. Do students receive frequent reading, field, or laboratory assignments, for which they are held accountable?

2. Do instructors assign grades based on examinations, papers, work projects, oral reports, and other suitable measures of pupil performance?

3. Are grades reported to parents, guardians, employers, or other responsible parties?

4. Are transcripts available to employers or similar institutions?

5. Does the course lead to a recognized degree, diploma, license, or certificate?

Meeting these criteria does not guarantee that nonprofit institutions qualify for the Sect. 110(1) privileges. Conversely, because of the vagueness in the law, these institutions may not need to meet the above tests to qualify. This grey area must be resolved by the courts. The courts cannot resolve this issue until a suitable case is introduced. The copyright proprietors have not sued a church or hospital for copyright infringements, other than infringements of music copyrights. However, in the first week in July, 1987, one law firm in New York sent forty cease-and-desist letters to summer camps for infringing video performances. Some of these camps were probably church operated. This could lead to suing infringers.

PERFORMANCES IN INDUSTRIAL TRAINING CENTERS

As noted above, all video performances outside the home must be licensed, except performances exempt by Sect. 110(1) for classes and Sect. 106(4) for business meetings. When the nonprofit element is removed, the Sect. 110(1) exemption is lost. Therefore, video performances in meetings and employee training programs must be licensed or offered under the business-meeting exemption discussed in the following chapter.

A clearcut exemption appears when training programs are offered at the work site by a college or school district. If all the students are enrolled at the school or college and all of the other requirements are met, video performances in an industrial classroom or laboratory may be exempt performances under Sect. 110(1). The training specialist should examine the conditions carefully to be sure all the requirements discussed in Chapter 2 are met.

A problem sometimes arises when firms offer training programs to handicapped or disadvantaged individuals as a community service. If the trainees are not employees and will not become employees at the end of the program, and the firm underwrites the cost of the program, video performances in the classroom may be exempt under Sect. 110(1), but care must be taken to insure that this is truly a nonprofit undertaking and all the conditions of that section are met. A copyright attorney should be consulted to be sure the program meets the requirements.

Classroom video performances in labor union training programs may qualify if the sponsoring agency, the union, is certified as a nonprofit agency, and the training program meets all the requirements of Sect. 110(1). If a union is

sued for a copyright infringement in a classroom performance, the decision may hinge on whether the training program was a well-structured educational endeavor, such as
a bricklaying course for apprentice bricklayers. On the
other hand, recreational courses offered as a fringe benefit
to union members and their families may not qualify. A
copyright attorney should be consulted to be certain the
requirements have been met.

TRAINING PROGRAMS OFFERED BY CONSULTANTS

The exemptions provided in Sect. 110(1) do not appear to apply to consultants who conduct training programs. That exemption applies only to non-profit agencies
and consultants offer a commercial service. Offering the
service to a nonprofit agency may not satisfy the requirement that the performance must be "in the course of . . .
[the] . . . teaching activities of a nonprofit educational institution."[16] An outside consultant would have difficulty
demonstrating that his or her services were part of the
regular instructional services of a school or college unless
he or she received a faculty appointment. On the other
hand, many training programs offered by consultants probably fit the business-meeting exemption discussed in the
following chapter.

CONCLUSION

Sect. 110(1) of the copyright law grants broad exemptions for performances of copyrighted works in face-to-face
instruction in nonprofit educational institutions. The law
clearly applies to schools, colleges, and universities. Part of
the law was written in vague terms and it is difficult to apply to educational programs conducted by other agencies.
Church, hospital, and industrial training specialists

should be cautious in applying Sect. 110(1) and Sect. 106(4) to their own situation. If there is any doubt about the application of the law to a given situation, it is best to consult an attorney who specializes in copyright matters and follow his or her advise.

CHAPTER 6:

THE BUSINESS-MEETING

EXEMPTION

Many video performances in meetings and staff-training programs in industry, government, and nonprofit agencies may be authorized under a little-studied aspect of Sect. 106(4). The definition of "publicly" in Sect. 101, when applied to Section 106(4), appears to authorize non-public performances in business firms, and in government and nonprofit agencies:

To perform or display a work "publicly" means—

(1) to perform or display it at a place open to the public or at any place where a substantial number of persons outside of a normal circle of a family and its social acquaintances is gathered. . . .[1]

The key phrase is "or at any place where a substantial number of persons outside of a normal circle of a family and its social acquaintances is gathered. . . ." The House of Representatives subcommittee report which accompanied the copyright act comments: "Routine meetings of businesses and governmental personnel would be excluded because they do not represent the gathering of a 'substantial number of persons'."[2]

The recent appellate court decision in the Nickelodeon case, described in previous chapters, discusses the definition of public performances in Sect. 101:

> Section 101 also states that to perform a work "publicly" means "[t]o perform . . . it at a place open to the public or at any place where a substantial number of persons outside of a normal circle of a family and its social acquaintances is gathered. The statute is written in the disjunctive, and thus two categories of paces can satisfy the definition of "to perform a work publicly." The first category is self-evident; it is "a place open to the public." The second category, commonly referred to as a semi-public place, is determined by the size and composition of the audience.[3]

This suggests a performance may be exempt if the performance is not open to the public, and the size and composition of the audience is restricted.

The pre-1965 copyright revision bills and the accompanying congressional committee reports are uninformative about this exemption. The 1965 copyright revision bill, committee reports, and the report of the Register of Copyrights indicate that this section of the bill was finalized in about 1965, at a time when many sections of the bill were finalized. Subsequent bills and congressional reports repeat the texts quoted above. It has been suggested that the specific reference to performances in business meetings in the house report were written to accompany a separate definition of non-public performances in a copyright revision bill. This speculation suggests that the specific exemption was removed from the bill but the commentary was inadvertently left in the congressional reports. The author has not found any evidence to support this contention and a Copyright Office attorney who is very familiar with this subject indicated she had no recollection of such an exemption in Sects. 106 or 110.

This issue received little attention since the Copyright Revision Act passed in 1976. It is not addressed in the major reference tool, *Nimmer on Copyright*, nor in the two leading case books. A recent search for legal periodical articles did not identify a single article on this subject.[4] This aspect of performance rights also has not been the subject of a lawsuit. As a result, this brief chapter is based almost entirely on two quotations, one from the copyright act and one from the congressional committee reports. Readers should recognize that this chapter is a preliminary exploration of the topic and should not assume it enunciates a well-established legal principle.

CONDITIONS FOR THE EXEMPTION

If a business-meeting exemption exists, it appears to apply to all businesses, government agencies, and non-profit agencies. Several conditions appear to be required:

1. The performance must not be accessible to the public.

2. Furthermore, the performances probably should not be accessible to anyone except employees, since performances to non-employees may make the performances accessible to the public.

3. Attendance at each performance must be limited to an insubstantial number of people, and

4. If the program is shown repeatedly, the attendance at all performances must be insubstantial.

The copyright act does not define substantial or insubstantial. Substantial has been defined in many court cases, but few of the definitions appear to have the remotest application to this use of the word. However, it may be helpful to examine two definitions that may reflect on the businees-meeting exemption:

> "Substantial" is a relative term, its measure to be gauged by all the circumstances surrounding the matter in reference to which the expression is used.[5]

> and

> "Substantial" is a relative term, the meaning of which is to be gauged by all the circumstances surrounding the transaction in reference to which the expression has been used, and it imports a considerable amount of value in opposition to that which is inconsequential or small.[6]

Lacking better direction, common sense must be applied. The exemption appears to apply equally to performances in for-profit and non-profit organizations and appears to include a variety of staff meetings and staff-training programs offered by a great variety of firms, government and nonprofit agencies, so long as the number in attendance is "insubstantial" and the performance is not accessible to the public. Restricting performances to employees may not be essential, but it seems like a safe limitation so that performances do not become accessible to the public.

EXAMPLES

The above requirements seem simple, yet their application is sure to raise many questions. A few hypothetical examples may be useful:

1. May a firm with one thousand employees perform videocassettes at an annual meeting for employees?

Probably not, as the number in attendance appears to be substantial.

2. May a firm with one thousand employees perform a videocassette at a series of small meetings that will eventually include most employees?

The performances at individual meetings may be acceptable because the attendance at any performance appears to be insubstantial. The question centers on the cumulative effect of repeated performances to small groups. If the aggregate number of viewers represent a substantial audience, the answer is no.

3. May a large firm show training programs to selected employees to improve their job skills?

Probably yes, if the total number of employees who see the program is insubstantial.

4. May a firm or agency perform copyrighted video programs to prospective employees?

Probably not, as attendance includes individuals who will not become employees, thus making the performances accessible to at least part of the general public.

5. May nonprofit agencies perform training programs to unpaid volunteers?

This is a difficult question, as volunteers are not employees and the number of volunteers may represent a substantial part of the community. If the number of volunteers who will see the program over several years is insubstantial, this may be an acceptable practice, but caution is advised.

6. May a college perform videocassettes to a small student organization (e.g., a French-Language Club)?

Probably not, as this exemption appears to apply to employees and not to students. Furthermore, the cumulative effect of repeated performances might be regarded as performances accessible to the public.

7. May a college perform videocassettes to train its student employees?

Probably yes, if attendance is limited to employees and is insubstantial.

8. May librarians view videocassettes to evaluate or catalog them?

Presumably yes, if attendance at single or sequential performances is limited to a small number of employees.

9. May a twelve-member, school, curriculum-evaluation committee perform thirty videocassettes to evaluate them for class use.

Presumably yes, if attendance is limited to a nonsubstantial number of employees. The number of titles they view to evaluate does not appear to be a significant issue.

These examples may help to define the business-meeting exemption as it is presently understood. Again, this exemption is based on one vague definition in the copyright act and one sentence in a congressional committee report. One cannot be assured of validity of the business-meeting exemption until the issue is addressed by the courts.

USING COPYRIGHTED VIDEOCASSETTES

CHAPTER 7:

COPYRIGHT CONTRACTS

When the film industry began, the print-oriented copyright law offered inadequate protection for films. To meet this problem, the studios used contracts or licenses to replace or supplement copyright protection. The practice soon spread to the ancillary film market, which includes schools, colleges, libraries, prisons, etc. Two key terms, licenses and contracts, are used here. *Black's Law Dictionary* defines a license as "A certificate or the document itself which gives permission."[1] It defines contract as "A promissory agreement between two or more persons that creates, modifies or destroys a legal relation."[2] In effect, a license to perform, transmit, or duplicate an audiovisual work is a contract granting a right reserved to the copyright proprietor. Although the terms license and contract have specific meanings, they appear to be used interchangeably in the industry and are used interchangeably in this book.

When the film industry began selling films under contract to schools, libraries, churches, hospitals, clubs, summer camps, and other nonprofit agencies, the contracts permitted purchasers to show films in certain environments, on condition that admission to the performances was free. These rights are usually called "non-theatrical public performance rights" or "audiovisual rights."

Today, almost all 16mm films are leased under a life-of-the-print contract that grants the purchaser the use of the film, for as long as it survives. Most life-of-the print contracts grant nontheatrical public performance rights. Videocassettes sold by educational film and video distributors are frequently leased under life-of-the-tape contracts that include nontheatrical public performance rights. Videocassettes distributed outside the educational and library markets are frequently sold outright, without performance rights. These tapes are usually labeled, "For home use only," which indicates performance rights were not included in the sale.

Most educational film and video distributors have a standard sales contract which appears in their catalogs. Many firms appear to have additional contracts covering transmission rights, duplication rights, and other situations. Catalogs and order forms usually state that the terms of the sales contract are binding on the purchaser. Similar wording appears in the fine print on invoices. As a result, purchasers are subject to the terms of these contracts, unless they negotiate alternate terms or include alternate purchase conditions on purchase orders. Film and video contracts include many conditions which should be clearly understood by purchasers.

CONDITIONS INCLUDED IN FILM AND VIDEO CONTRACTS

Films and videocassettes are normally sold under contracts or licenses. These documents frequently include the following conditions:

1. Some contracts have a specific duration, usually for one year, and must be renegotiated at the end of the term. The

ideal specific-duration license has a multiyear life or includes a renewal option, with a discount for continued use of the product. Film and video duplication contracts sometimes run for five years and are renewable at a discount.

A life-of-the-product contract is fairly simple. If the client can make the product last ten years, the contract has a ten year life. If the product is lost, stolen, or destroyed the day it is purchased, the contract expires that day. Some contracts include discounts for replacing lost, stolen, or destroyed copies.

2. All contracts are limited to specific titles. This is necessary as the price is based on the amount of product covered. More importantly, distributors must limit their contracts to the products they are authorized to license. The day of the blanket license has passed.

3. Almost all contracts authorize in-house performances, which is the essential element for public library licenses. This authorization is not needed for most classroom performances in schools and colleges, but it is essential for non-classroom performances, such as lunch-hour and after-school showings and showings in lounges.

4. Some contracts authorize loaning the product for use outside the purchasing institution. Libraries already have the right to loan materials for outside use under Section 109(a) of the copyright act, so they should not undermine that right by purchasing circulation rights. Contracts can avoid the appearance of granting Section 109(a) rights by including the following statement:

> The client's right under Title 17, *U.S. Code*, Sect. 109(a), to loan copyrighted materials to its patrons is

not subject to nor affected by this contract.

The law tends to enforce business customs. If contracts routinely grant rights clients already posses, the rights may be undermined by the custom. Although libraries should be wary of signing contracts that grant the right to loan materials, they may agree to restrict those rights to reduce the fee.

5. None of the contracts the author examined specifically excluded performances authorized under Sect. 110(1), but that remains a viable option. A reader called the author's attention to a firm that refuses to sell its videocassettes to schools, colleges, or libraries. Its cassette labels state that the videocassettes may not be shown in libraries and classrooms. This firm is a subsidiary or licensee of a well-known producer of children's animated films. The producer sells its films, videocassettes, filmstrips, and slide sets directly to the institutional market with nontheatrical public performance rights. Some of its programs also are sold in the home market, but without performance rights. The producer does not want its home-market distributor competing with its institutional sales, since programs offered in the home market sell for less than the same program sold in the institutional market. This does not appear to be an effort to undermine educators Sect. 110(1) rights. Rather, it is an example of careful attention to the two-tiered (home and institutional) videocassette market.

6. Contracts always specify fees. Expensive audiovisual materials, including film and video, are frequently subject to price negotiation, so don't accept the first price quoted on large sales. Prices should be based on the nature or extent of use. Clearly, a small public library with one videocassette player and two thousand cardholders should not pay the same fee as a large library with two hundred

machines and thirty thousand cardholders. Likewise, a small school district or college should not pay as much as a large institution for non-classroom showings. Most vendors offer a variety of rates to accommodate the number of people served. When MGM/UA began selling college and university residence hall performance licenses, the fee was usually one dollar, per pupil, per year, but some colleges negotiated lower fees. Some clients have negotiated lower fees in return for restricting the number of performances permitted during the life of the contract. (This might be appropriate for a hospital or residence hall license.) A client leasing multiple titles or multiple copies may want to include an early-return-for-credit provision, to obtain credit for low-use items, or to exchange them for new titles.

Film and video duplication licenses are usually based on the retail price of the 16mm film. The fees range from ten to fifty percent of the price of the film, depending on the duration of use (i.e., one year versus life of the tape) and the number of copies to be made.

7. Almost all contracts prohibit commercial and theatrical showings. This is perfectly reasonable, as the licensor does not want free school and library performances competing with local theatrical performances. One license included a troublesome requirement that all showings be "private." Private is not defined in the copyright law, but an opposite term, "publicly" is defined in the law and it precludes most performances outside the home. Contracts which limit showings to "private" performances should be rejected unless the term is satisfactorily defined in the contract.

The videocassette sales contract for a Southern California PBS station includes the following condition in its videocassette sales contract: "Said copy is licensed to Licensee solely for personal reference and audition purposes. . . . Licensee . . . shall not exhibit or televise said copy." The terms "personal reference" and "audition" are not defined, but the phrase "shall not exhibit" prohibits performances to a public school class or an individual library patron. This contract term should never be accepted.

8. Most contracts are limited to non-paying performances. The sale of nontheatrical public performance rights is traditionally based on free admission to all showings, so few distributors can or will change this practice. This limitation may prohibit clients from charging rental fees for videocassettes. Libraries that charge rental fees should be alert to this requirement.

Contracts which authorize admission fees usually specify the receipts be divided between the distributor and the client. (One contract specifies a 50-50 split of the gate receipts, payable within fifteen days of the showing, in addition to the licensing fee.)

9. Many contracts restrict rentals and loans outside the purchasing institution. Some contracts prohibit group or consortium purchases. Others charge a "sub-rental authorization fee" to permit rentals outside the purchasing institution. One firm charges one hundred dollars or twenty-five percent of the purchase price, whichever is greater, for sub-rental authorization. Another firm authorizes state-wide rentals of its 16mm films without additional charge, but charges an additional fee for rentals outside the state.

Because of the growing number of distributors that restrict rentals of films and videocassettes, some institutions include a purchase condition in their orders that authorize rentals. The following statement could be included in purchase orders: "Purchase contingent on the right to loan materials to non-profit agencies in [state or region] and charge a fee sufficient to recover costs." Costs are not defined here. It might cover the cost of shipping and handling, or it could include shipping and handling, plus an amount sufficient to amortize the purchase price over the product's useful lifespan.

10. Many contracts sold to public libraries prohibit school and college use or restrict showings to classroom performances. Performances at fraternities, sororities, residence-hall lounges, and other school and college events deprive distributors of a substantial income. These restrictions are included in contracts to stop this common but illegal practice. This clause can create problems if an infringing performance is made from a film or videocassette borrowed from a school, college, or public library. This restriction should be examined carefully to minimize liability for unsupervised performances by patrons.

Some contracts for theatrical films and videocassettes specify the rooms or buildings where the performances will be given. They may also restrict the size of the video screens or monitors. (One contract specifies that videocassettes will not be shown on screens larger than twenty-five inches measured diagonally.)

11. Almost all contracts prohibit editing or copying. This is to be expected, as those rights are sold separately. Many distributors include that statement in contracts because they do not hold duplication rights. One firm attempts to prevent altering or editing of programs by requiring clients to perform or transmit the programs in their entirety. Licenses to duplicate films and videocassettes are available from many distributors. Charles W. Vlcek states that the

average cost for a license to duplicate a film to videocassette is about one hundred dollars.[3] Many duplication licenses include detailed requirements about statements that must appear on labels attached to videocassette copies. A few vendors send their own labels and require that they be attached to copies made under the contract.

12. Broadcast and transmission rights are almost always sold separately. Many distributors do not control the broadcast rights for their products but they can negotiate microwave and cable transmission rights. Institutions that buy films and videocassettes should insist on receiving transmission rights at the time of purchase that match the institution's transmission capabilities. It is much easier and cheaper to acquire those rights at the time of purchase than it is to negotiate them later.

The price for closed-circuit transmission rights varies widely. One distributor automatically grants in-building transmission rights at no additional charge; broader transmission rights are available for a fee. Many distributors include in-building and campus-wide closed-circuit transmission rights free of charge upon request. Other firms charge ten to fifteen percent of the purchase price of the product, which is probably negotiable. Charles W. Vlcek states that where fees are charged, the average cost of a life-of-the-tape, closed-circuit transmission licenses is about one hundred dollars.[4]

13. Most contracts prohibit advertising performances, except through in-house announcements. A few contracts only prohibit paid advertising. This is a well-established restriction and it seems reasonable, since the studios do not want school, college, and library performances competing with theatrical performances. A few clients have negotiated a clause permitting low-level announcements in

school newspapers or in handouts distributed outside the institution.

14. Specific-duration contracts for videocassettes frequently specify that the product must be returned at the end of the contract term. This clause is not not frequently found in the film contracts. Failure to return the product for any reason frequently results in a penalty. (One contract specified a $1,000-per-videocassette penalty.) Library materials are sometimes lost or stolen, so clients should insist on an exemption for lost or stolen materials.

Specific-duration contracts frequently require the client to return the product at the end of the term or destroy the product and certify the destruction to the distributor. A few life-of-the-product contracts also require the client to return the product when it is no longer useable or destroy the product and certify the destruction to the distributor. A few life-of-the-product contracts also require the client to certify theft or loss of a product to the distributor. These conditions require the client to establish appropriate control procedures in their inventory or accession files. These conditions are appropriate for specific-duration contracts but they seem unnecessarily burdensome for life-of-the-product contracts. Clients may want to negotiate to exclude that requirement.

The return provision also should allow time to recover overdue items, withdraw them from accession files, and ship them to the lessor. A thirty-day grace period should be sufficient. Without a grace period, it may be necessary to withdraw the videocassettes before the contract expires to avoid paying the penalty.

Single-showing and weekly rentals usually specify substantial late-return fees. The fee may be equal to the rental rate. If a videocassette is returned late because the client sent it by mail instead of by express service, the late-return fee applies.

15. Many videocassette contracts indicate the vendor will replace defective videocassettes without charge, but damages caused by the customer or its patrons will be repaired at the customer's expense. This could be expensive, so a price schedule for this service should be included in the contract. Clients might consider negotiating a clause authorizing an early return of damaged copies for partial credit, in lieu of paying for repairs.

16. Film contracts should include a guarantee that replacement footage will be available on sixty days notice, in one-hundred-foot increments, for a period of ten years. Failure to comply with this clause should trigger a penalty clause requiring the vendor to refund twenty-five percent of the purchase price of the film.

17. Performance contracts for feature films sometimes require clients to make regular (usually monthly) reports of the number of performances for each title. Clients sometimes complain about these "nuisance reports," but these reports are a time-consuming "nuisance" to distributors, too. This contractual requirement is usually dictated by studio executives who are accustomed to receiving frequent reports of theatrical bookings. The distributors' payments to the studios are sometimes based on these reports.

18. Penalty clauses are routinely included in contracts in the event either party fails to fulfill its contractual obligations. Some contracts authorize the vendor to seize the product and impose monetary penalties if purchasers fail to observe the terms of the the the contracts. This condition is

rarely invoked, but it should be carefully considered. Penalty clauses are a normal part of contracts, but clients should require a balance in these provisions to protect their own interests. Assurances by sales personnel that the company never invokes the penalties must be disregarded.

19. Traditional boilerplate is included in contracts to limit liabilities, to guarantee fulfillment of the terms, and to assure effective communication. Clients should seek a balance in the boilerplate. If the client must maintain a certain level of insurance or notify the vendor of an event via registered mail, similar or balancing provisions should be included. Public libraries and educational institutions should consider a clause protecting them from liability for illegal use of the materials. This will not be granted easily, or it may be granted in return for substantial restrictions on the use of the materials.

Plain-English licenses are not terribly difficult to understand, but beware of unfathomable legalese, it may conceal a nasty trap. Always assume film and videocassette contracts are written in the distributor's favor and must be treated cautiously. If a proposed contract is difficult to understand, have it reviewed by an institutional attorney, and don't let the attorney dismiss the issue with the statement, "its not important; don't worry about it." A sales contract which unnecessarily restricts the use of the product, or contains unusual requirements, should be sent to the author, in care of the publisher, so it can be treated in a future edition of this work.

PAPER LICENSES

Educators frequently say they want to buy an inexpensive annual blanket license that will authorize performance, duplication, and transmission of all the films and videocassettes they own. Alas, Aesop's goose no longer lays golden eggs. But one should not despair, the next best thing may be a "paper license." The name is puzzling, as all licenses are on paper. The term probably was generated in the film industry, which is noted for its colorful terminology. Regardless of its etymology, paper licenses are easy to understand. They provide nontheatrical public performance rights for a specified list of titles. The client acquires the programs from other sources, usually from discount distributors.

Paper licenses for non-theatrical films and videocassettes (e.g., documentaries and instructional programs) are offered by many firms, so there is no central clearinghouse. Paper licenses for most theatrical films are handled by three firms. Two of the firms, Films, Inc. and Swank Audio-Visuals, specialize in distributing feature films to nonprofit agencies. (Their addresses are in Appendix C.)

The latest development in paper licenses for theatrical films comes from the Motion Picture Licensing Corporation of America (MPLC). It was established as "the video ASCAP" in 1985 and began selling licenses in July, 1987. It secures nontheatrical public performance licenses from many studios, then resells the rights to public libraries, hospitals, nursing homes, churches, clubs, hotels, prisons, corporations, day care facilities, limousine services, and other organizations. (Colleges and school districts are not currently included in its marketing plan.) An MPLC paper license is expected to cover videocassette and videodisc copies of theatrical films produced by most of the major and mini-major studios, plus many small studios. At the time of writing, MPLC had not released its rate card or list of titles, so it remains to be seen if this service will be more economical, comprehensive, or convenient than licenses available from other firms. (MPLC's contract appears in Appendix B; its address appears in Appendix C.)

CHAPTER 8:

WARNING NOTICES

Several years ago, the Motion Picture Association of America Film Security Office issued a "warning notice" about performing rights for home use only videocassettes. The warning notice caused great consternation among educators because of a reference to schools. Because of the confusion, MPAA withdrew its warning notice and urged film and video distributors to do the same. That issue was treated at length in the first edition of this book. Although the MPAA warning notice has been withdrawn, educators continue to question its validity and impact. Those persistent questions will be answered here at the risk of offending MPAA members who may think the author is immercifully beating a dead horse.

To repeat what was said before, the MPAA Warning Notice is accurate insofar as it describes proprietors' rights and home-use rights, but it is flawed because it:

    A. uses, without explanation, a widely misunderstood quotation from Section 106 of the House and Senate Reports, and

    B. lacks information about educators' rights under Sect. 110(1).

The widely misunderstood quotation appears in the second sentence of the following quotation from the Warning Notice:

> The U.S. Copyright Act grants to the copyright owner the *exclusive* right, among others, "to perform the copyrighted work publicly." Even "performances in 'semipublic' places such as clubs, lodges, factories, summer camps, and schools are 'public performances' subject to copyright control." (Citations within the text omitted.)[1]

Questions center on the second quotation. Those parts of the reports were clearly not intended to prohibit performances in face-to-face teaching, but to describe a new feature in Sect. 106 enabling copyright proprietors to control performances. The 1909 copyright act gave proprietors little control over nonprofit performances of nondramatic works, so public radio and television stations, schools, and clubs used nondramatic works without permission and without paying fees. The new copyright act reduced the nonprofit loophole, without completely closing it, so authors, composers, filmmakers, and others could be compensated for the use of their works. The confusing quotation, above, is part of a long description of the proposed right to regulate public and semipublic performances. That part of the congressional report is given here in its entirety, with emphasis for the portion quoted in the MPAA Warning Notice:

> Under clause (1) of the definition of "publicly" in section 101, a performance or display is "public" if it takes place "at a place open to the public or at any place where a substantial number of persons outside of a normal circle of a family and its social acquaintances is gathered." One of the principal purposes of the

definition was to make clear that, contrary to the decision in *Metro-Goldwyn-Mayer Distributing Corp.* v. *Wyatt*, 21 C.O. Bull. 203 (D. Md. 1932), **performances in "semipublic" places such as clubs, lodges, factories, summer camps, and schools are "public performances" subject to copyright control.** The term "a family" in this context would include an individual living alone, so that a gathering confined to the individual's social acquaintances would normally be regarded as private. Routine meetings of businesses and governmental personnel would be excluded because they do not represent the gathering of a "substantial number of persons."[2]

When read in context, it is evident this confusing quotation was not intended to undermine educators' rights, but to describe the proprietors' new rights to control performances. The question then arises—if the statement was not designed to deny educators' rights to performances in face-to-face teaching, why are schools mentioned here? The sentence appears to have originated in the *Supplementary Report of the Register of Copyrights on the General Revision of the U.S. Copyright Law: 1965 Revision Bill*[7] and was repeated in subsequent reports. The Register's report provides ample evidence the Register and congressional leaders wanted the new copyright act to give copyright proprietors broad rights to control performances and displays. The report also indicated, in other chapters, a decision by the Register and congressional leaders to exempt performances and displays in face-to-face teaching.[4] Both points were well established by 1965, and the language in the two sections of the bill and the reports was little changed in the twelve years remaining until the act passed in 1976.

There may be several reasons "schools" appeared in Sect. 106 of the congressional and Copyright Office reports. First, the Register's comments on the teaching exemption express a concern the exemption might be misused for entertainment or cultural events held at schools.[5] Since the copyright bill contained a substantial change in the proprietors' control over nonprofit performances, it seemed important to state clearly that performances and displays in schools could fall within the proprietors' right to regulate performances and displays. It is unfortunate the Register did not include a qualifying phrase at that point in the report referring to exempt performances in face-to-face teaching.

A second possible cause for this apparent conflict is the fact that various sections of the bills and reports sometimes appeared to exist independently of each other, so statements in one section sometimes failed to reflect statements in another section of the bill or report. This is apparent in the confusion over educational broadcasters rights in Sect. 110(2) and the right to make ephemeral recordings in Sect. 112. (Educators sometimes read Sect. 112 in isolation and assume they are authorized to reproduce sound recordings for class use.)

Speculation about the reason for including "school" in the quotation is incidental to the key point—which is more important, the law or the congressional reports? Congressional reports (often called legislative history) accompanying bills are significant explanations of legislative intent. They are frequently cited to clarify difficult or confusing points, but they do not have the force of law, so they cannot overturn the law. When the law and legislative reports are in conflict, the law is supreme. Accordingly, the confusing quotation in the MPAA warning notice does not reduce educators rights under Sect. 110(1).

As a result of the confusion caused by the MPAA notice, the Film Security Office stopped distributing the warning notice, and replaced it with several new pamphlets, including: *Film & Video Piracy: Public Performance, Unauthorized Exhibitions of Pre-Recorded Videocassettes*. The pamphlet is a brief statement of the copyright proprietors performance rights in prerecorded videocassettes. It accurately states it is an infringement to perform a videocassette "in non-classroom use at schools and universities, such as in a residence hall common room accessible to the entire dormitory population regardless of whether an admission fee is charged to enter the establishment."[6] This pamphlet and several others are available free from the MPAA Film Security Office. (Address in Appendix C.)

WARNING LABELS ON VIDEOCASSETTES

In about 1978, several major motion picture distributors began displaying warning labels on videocassettes sold in the home market. The text of the labels varies from firm-to-firm, but the following is typical:

Licensed only for non-commercial private exhibition in homes. Any public performance, other use, or copying is strictly prohibited. All rights under copyright reserved.

FBI WARNING

Federal law provides severe civil and criminal penalties for unauthorized reproduction, distribution, or exhibition of copyrighted motion pictures and video tapes (Title 17, United States Code, Sections 501 and 506). The Federal Bureau of Investigation investigates allegations of criminal copyright infringement, (Title 17, United States Code, Section 506).[7]

The Consortium of University Film Centers distributes a similar notice to its members which they attach to film cans and videocassettes. The notice displays the logo of the Federal Bureau of Investigation and states:

WARNING

Federal law provides severe civil and criminal penalties for the unauthorized reproduction, distribution or exhibition of copyrighted motion pictures, video tapes or video discs.

Criminal copyright infringement is investigated by the FBI and may constitute a felony with a maximum penalty of up to five years in prison and/or $250,000 fine.[8]

In 1979, the American Library Association asked its attorney, Newton N. Minow (FCC chairman, 1961-63) to comment on using videodiscs labeled for home use only in public libraries. Minow's response raised doubts about the power of the home-use-only label to prevent libraries and other institutions from loaning videodiscs for home use or performing them in private rooms. Although his comments address the label issue, they appear to apply to warning labels on all videorecordings:

[I]individual use of the video discs in the library or at home would not constitute an infringement of the copyright owner's exclusive right to perform the work publicly. . . .

While there is thus little likelihood that a library's use of the video discs would constitute copyright infringement, it is possible that a copyright owner would attempt to prevent such use based on a contract theory. "For Home Use Only" could be read as simply a restatement of the copyright owner's exclusive performance rights as discussed above, or as a condition of the sale. If the video discs are sold to libraries by the manufacturer or his agent, it is unlikely that the legend could be held to be a condition of sale since library use would clearly be contemplated by the parties. Furthermore, there is some case law which holds such restrictions invalid. In *RCA Mfg. Co., Inc. v. Whiteman*, 114 F.2d 86, 90 (2nd Cir. 1940), the court held that the legend on records, "Not Licensed for Radio Broadcast" constituted an invalid "servitude upon the records," analogous to resale price restrictions and other antitrust violations. *See also, Universal Film Mfg. Co. v. Copperman*, 218 Fed. 577 (2nd Cir. 1914) [condition on sale of film that it should not be sold or hired out outside of country where purchased held invalid.] In both these cases, the courts found restrictions on use inconsistent with the concept of an outright sale. If possession of the video discs was transferred by lease or license, such restrictions possibly would be appropriate and legally binding.[9]

Burton H. Hanft, MPAA's copyright attorney, was asked to comment on Mr. Minow's letter:

You requested comments on the significance of the "for home use only" label which our clients affix to videocassettes and discs (herein called "cassettes") of their copyrighted motion pictures. . . .

The purposes of such labels is probably an attempt by our clients to inform purchasers of a basic concept in copyright law: that the transfer of title of a cassette does not grant the purchaser any right to perform the cassette publicly. . . . The label affixed to a cassette is intended to correct that mistaken impression. . . .[10]

Although Mr. Hanft does not challenge Mr. Minow's statement that labels are not binding, he does not advocate that position either. One should not attach too much significance to that, as it may have been prompted by a perception the proprietors have a better basis for regulating performances under Sects. 101 and 106, especially as they were applied in the Redd Horne and Nickelodeon decisions.

The question remains, do the labels limit the use of videocassettes in libraries and other institutions? Probably not. Evidence has not been presented to suggest the labels constitute binding contracts on purchasers, so buyers may be safe in that regard, but that begs the central issue. Prescriptive language on adhesive labels is one of several approaches copyright proprietors use to protect their right to control public performances. But labels are mere auxiliaries in this conflict. The proprietors' rights stem from Sects. 101 and 106, the proprietors' main weapons for enforcing their rights. Placing warning labels on videocassettes and distributing informational pamphlets provide evidence of the proprietors good faith efforts to inform infringers of their errors. Ignorance of the law is not an acceptable defense, but a substantial lack of information about the seriousness of one's offenses may enable certain infringers to mitigate monetary damages. The proprietors do not want that excuse to dull the sharp edge of the legal tools at their disposal. In short, the "label issue" is a side issue in the larger conflict over users' and proprietors' rights.

NOTES

Introduction to the First Edition

1. Motion Picture Association of America. Film Security Office. "Warning 'For Home Use Only' Means Just That." Hollywood, CA: the association, n.d., broadside. (Hereafter: MPAA Warning Notice.)

2. U.S. House of Representatives, *Report No. 94-1476*, Sect. 106. (Hereafter: House Report.)

Introduction to the Second Edition

1. For a thorough treatment of videotaping off the air, see: E.R. Sinofsky, *Off-Air Videotaping in Education: Copyright Issues, Decisions, Implications,* (New York: Bowker, 1984); and R.D. Billings, "Off-The-Air Videorecording, Face-To-face Teaching, and the 1976 Copyright Act," *Northern Kentucky Law Review,* Vol. 4, (1977), pp. 225-251.

Key Terminology

1. *United States Code,* Title 17, "Copyrights," Sect. 101. (Hereafter: Copyright Act.)

2. Ibid.

Chapter 1

1. Copyright Act, Sect. 106.

2. *Columbia Pictures* v. *Redd Horne,* U.S. District Court for the Western District of Pennsylvania. No. 83-0016, July 28, 1983. (568 FSupp. 494)

3. Telephone call to the Clerk of the Court, Nov. 17, 1983.

4. *Columbia Pictures* v. *Redd Horne,* U.S. Court of Appeals for the Third Circuit. No. 83-5786. Nov. 23, 1984. (749 F2d 154, 224)

5. *Columbia Pictures* v. *Aveco*, U.S. District Court for the Middle District of Pennsylvania. No. 84-0774, June 28, 1985. (612 FSupp. 315)

6. *Columbia Pictures* v. *Aveco*, U.S. Court of Appeals for the Third Circuit. No. 85-5608. Sept. 4, 1986. (800 Fed2d 59)

Chapter 2

1. Copyright Act, Sect. 106.

2. Ibid., Sect. 101.

Chapter 3

1. Copyright Act, Sect. 110.

2. House Report, Sect. 110.

3. Ibid.

4. Ibid.

5. Ibid.

6. U.S. House of Representatives. *Copyright Law Revision, Part 6 — Supplementary Report of the Register of Copyrights on the General Revision of the U.S. Copyright Law: 1965* (Washington, D.C.: Government Printing Office, 1965), p. 37. (Hereafter: Register's Report.)

7. Copyright Act, Sect. 110(2).

8. Ibid., Sect. 101.

9. House Report, Sect. 110.

10. Copyright Act, Sect. 110(4).

Chapter 4

1. Copyright Act, Sect. 110(1)

2. House Report, Sect. 110.

3. *Columbia Pictures* v. *Redd Horne*, U.S. District Court for the Western District of Pennsylvania. No. 83-0016, July 28, 1983. (568 FSupp. 494)

4. *Columbia Pictures* v. *Aveco*, U.S. District Court for the Middle District of Pennsylvania. No. 84-0774, June 28, 1985. (612 FSupp. 315)

5. *Columbia Pictures* v. *Aveco*, U.S. Court of Appeals for the Third Circuit. No. 85-5608. Sept. 4, 1986. (800 Fed2d 59)

6. *Columbia Pictures* v. *Professional Real Estate Investors*, U.S. District Court for the Central District of California. No. 83-2594. (DC CD Cal 1986)

7. Mary Hutchings Reed, *The Copyright Primer for Librarians and Educators*, Chicago: American Library Association; and Washington: National Education Association, 1987, p. 33.

8. Mary Hutchings Reed and Debra Stanek, "Library and Classroom Use of Copyrighted Videotapes and Computer Software." A four-page centerfold in the February, 1986 *American Libraries*. The document is available separately; single copies are free when the request includes a stamped, self-addressed envelope. Hutchings Reed is a partner in Sidley & Austin and counsel to the American Library Assoc. Stanek was a senior at the University of Chicago Law School.

9. Reed, *The Copyright Primer*, p. iv.

10. Debra J. Stanek, "Videotapes, Computer Programs, and the Library," *Information Technology and Libraries*, March, 1986, pp. 42-54.

11. William F. Patry, *The Fair Use Privilege in Copyright Law*, Washington: Bureau of National Affairs, 1985.

12. Reed, *The Copyright Primer*, p. 34.

13. Persons present were: Ivan Bender, AIME Counsel; Charles Benton, Public Media Inc.; Tom Ciesielka, Films, Inc.; Joe Elliott, Coronet/MTI and President of AIME; Thomas Galvan, ALA; Allen Green, Films, Inc.; Mara Karduck, ALA-Carnegie Video Project; Edgar McLarin, ALA Publishing; Sally Mason, ALA-Carnegie Video Project; Mary Hutchings Reed, ALA Counsel; Harvey Shapiro, MPAA Counsel; Michael Stickney, Films, Inc.

14. *The Video Librarian*, a monthly newsletter published by Randy Pitman, 2219 East View Ave., NE, Bremerton, WA 98310. $35 per year.

15. Henry Campbell Black, *Black's Law Dictionary: Definitions of the Terms and Phrases of American and English Jurisprudence, Ancient and Modern*, St. Paul: West, 1968, Rev. 4th ed., p. 484.

16. Copyright Act, Sect. 109(a).

17. House Report, Sect. 109.

18. Copyright Act, Sect. 109(b)(1).

Chapter 5

1. Copyright Act, Sect. 101.

2. House Report, Sect. 106.

3. Register's Report, p. 37.

4. U.S. House of Representatives, 100th Cong., 1st Sess. H.R. 2429, May 14, 1987.

5. Telephone interviews with Hazel Atherton of P.A.L.M.S, Susan Kaplan of Congressman Glickman's office, Marybeth Peters of the Copyright Office, Tom Ciesielka of Films, Inc., and Karen Mitchell of St. Francis Hospital.

6. *Columbia Pictures* v. *Aveco,* U.S. Court of Appeals for the Third Circuit. No. 85-5608. Sept. 4, 1986. (800 Fed2d 59)

7. House Report, Sect. 110.

8. *American Management Associations* v. *Assessor of Town of Madison,* 406 N.Y.S.2d 583, 585, 63A.D.2d 1102.

9. *Board of Directors of Fort Dodge Independent School Dist.* v. *Board of Sup'rs of Webster County,* 293 N.W.38, 40, 228 Iowa 544.

10. *Imbergamo* v. *Barclay,* 352 N.Y.S2d 337, 341, 77 Misc 2d 188.

11. *Circle Pines Center* v. *Orangeville Tp.,* 302 N.W.2d 917, 920 103 Mich.App. 593.

12. In re Goetz' Estate, 218 N.E.2d 483, 485, 8 Ohio Misc. 143.

13. House Report, Sect. 110.

14. Register's Report, p. 37.

15. Melville B. Nimmer, *Nimmer on Copyright: A Treaties on the Law of Literary, Musical and Artistic Property, and the Protection of Ideas,* (New York: M. Bender, 1963-), Sect. 8.15 [8][3]. Looseleaf.

16. Copyright Act, Sect 110(1).

Chapter 6

1. Copyright Act, Sect. 101.

2. House Report, Sect. 106.

3. *Columbia Pictures* v. *Aveco*, U.S. Court of Appeals for the Third Circuit. No. 85-5608. Sept. 4, 1986. (800 Fed2d 59)

4. "LegalTrac" searched July 13, 1987. The database covers legal journals published in the past ten years.

5. *Robinson* v. *North American Life & Cas. Co.*, App., 30 Cal. Rptr. 57, 60.

6. Application of Scroggin, Cal. App., 229 P.2d 489, 491.

Chapter 7

1. Henry Campbell Black, *Black's Law Dictionary*, p. 1067.

2. Ibid, p. 394.

3. Charles W. Vlcek, "Institutional Copyright Policy Regulating Video Use" in *Video Copyright Permissions*, Friday Harbor, WA: Copyright Information Services, 1988, from a manuscript copy of the chapter.

4. Ibid.

Chapter 8

1. MPAA Warning Notice.

2. House Report, Sect. 106.

3. Register's Report, pp. 23-24.

4. Ibid. pp. 32-34.

5. Ibid. pp. 33.

6. Motion Picture Association of America. Film Security Office. *Film & Video Piracy: Public Performance, Unauthorized Exhibitions of Prerecorded Videocassettes.* (New York: the association, 1986), unpaged.

7. Label on *Elephant Man*, Paramount Home Video, 1980. [VHS videocassette]

8. Consortium of University Film Centers, "Copyright labels order form," one page, n.d.

9. Newton N. Minow to Robert Wedgeworth, April 23, 1979

10. Burton H. Hanft to Jerome K. Miller, August 12, 1983

USING COPYRIGHTED VIDEOCASSETTES

APPENDICES

APPENDIX A:
LETTER REQUESTING BLANKET PERMISSION

Letterhead
Date

Sales Manager
Video distributor
Address
City, state zip

Dear . . . :

This library attempts to observe the copyright law in the services it provides to its patrons. These services include showing copyrighted videocassettes distributed by your firm in library carrels, viewing rooms, and auditoriums. Questions have recently been raised about the legality of showing videocassettes in public libraries. All showings in this library are given free of charge.

Until this question is resolved, this library has adopted a policy of limiting its purchases of copyrighted videocassettes to titles supplied by firms which provide written permission to perform the videocassettes in the library.

Attached is a list of the videocassettes we own which are distributed by your firm. Will you please send me a letter authorizing free, nonprofit library showings of these titles and other titles we purchase from you in the future.

Sincerely, etc.

Enclosure: List of titles

APPENDIX B:

Motion Picture Licensing Corporation
2777 Summer Street, Stamford, CT 06905
(203) 353-1600

Umbrella License Agreement

This letter — when (1) signed by you in the space provided at the bottom, (2) signed in the space provided in the Appendix, and (3) returned to us with a check for the agreed license fee shall constitute a license agreement between Motion Picture Licensing Corporation ("MPLC") and _____ ("you").

The purpose of this license agreement is to allow you to "publicly perform," as that term is used in Sections 101 and 106 of Title 17, United States Code, copyrighted pre-recorded video cassettes and videodiscs which are otherwise by law for home use only.

1. MPLC hereby grants you a non-exclusive license to publicly perform certain pre-recorded home video cassettes and videodiscs in your facility, under the terms and conditions specified in this license agreement.

2. MPLC warrants and represents that it has secured the appropriate rights, under the U.S. Copyright Act, Title 17, United States code, to grant the license contained in this agreement.

3. The term of this license agreement shall be one year, commencing on _____ and terminating on _____.

4. The facility at which the public performances authorized by this agreement are to take place is _____ _____, located at _____, and it is understood and agreed that the sole purpose of such public performances is to _____. It is further understood and agreed that the facility has a capacity of _____, that the audience will be limited to _____, that no specific titles will ever be advertised to the general public, and that no admission or other fee will be charged to the audience. Only the public performances specified in this paragraph are authorized by this license agreement.

5. The agreed license fee for the full term of this license agreement is $_____, which amount is payable to MPLC immediately upon signature and return of this letter.

6. The specific titles which may be publicly performed by you under this license agreement are motion pictures produced and/or distributed by the motion picture companies listed in the Appendix to this letter, which motion pictures appear on the home video labels specified adjacent to the name of each listed motion picture company. It is understood and agreed that, because MPLC or its motion picture company licensors may not possess that appropriate rights to certain individual titles or because those rights may expire during the term of this license agreement, MPLC may send you from time to time legally binding notices that certain individual titles cannot be or may no longer be publicly performed under this license agreement.

7. You may publicly perform the specific titles covered by this license agreement by means of lawfully manufac-

tured pre-recorded home video cassettes and videodiscs of those titles, acquired by you from any legitimate source of your choice. It is understood by you that the responsibility for obtaining such home video cassettes and videodiscs is yours, and that the costs of acquiring such home video cassettes and videodiscs are to be borne solely by you and are separate and distinct from the agreed public performance license fee specified in Paragraph 5 of this license agreement.

8. You may not duplicate, edit or otherwise modify the home video cassettes and videodiscs obtained by you for public performance purposes under this agreement. It is also understood by you that this license agreement does not authorize you to use for public performance purposes copies of titles covered by this agreement which have been videotaped off any form of television.

9. Any separate fees which may be due to music publishers, or collection societies for music publishers, for the right to publicly perform, the music contained in any of the motion pictures covered by this license agreement are solely your responsibility and are not the responsibility of MPLC.

10. This agreement may not be assigned by you, but may be assigned by MPLC.

11. Any notices which you or MPLC send to each other shall be sent, postage prepaid, to the addresses indicated on the first page of this letter.

12. MPLC reserves the right, exercisable upon 30 days prior written notice, to terminate this license agreement on account of any breach by you of its terms and conditions. In the event of such termination, there shall be no

refund of the agreed license fee. A waiver by MPLC or by you of any specific breach by the other shall not constitute a waiver of prior or subsequent breaches.

13. You acknowledge by the signature appearing at the bottom of this letter and on the Appendix that this license agreement has been duly and validly authorized, and constitutes a legal, valid and binding obligation upon you and is enforceable by its terms and conditions.

14. Any and all rights not granted to you in this license agreement are expressly reserved to MPLC and/or its motion picture company licensors.

15. This letter and its Appendix contain the full and complete agreement between MPLC and you, and shall be construed in accordance with the laws of the United States and the State of Connecticut.

This letter and its Appendix are enclosed in duplicate original form. After signature, one copy should be retained by you for your records and the other copy should be returned to MPLC along with your check for the agreed license fee specified in Paragraph 5 of this license agreement.

[Signature lines omitted]

APPENDIX C

DIRECTORY

The following firms and associations were identified in the book:

Films, Inc.
5547 N. Ravenswood Ave.
Chicago, IL 60640-1199

Phone: (800) 323-4222, Ex. 42
or (312) 878-2600, Ex. 42

Motion Picture Association of America
1133 Avenue of the Americas
New York, NY 10036.

Phone: (212) 840-6161

Motion Picture Licensing Corporation
2777 Summer Street
Stamford, CT 06905

Phone: (203) 353-1600

Swank Audio-Visuals Inc.
2800 Market St.
St. Louis, MO 63103

Phone: (314) 534-1940

APPENDIX D

APPELLATE COURT DECISION IN
COLUMBIA PICTURES V. *AVECO*

Columbia Pictures Industries, Inc., Embassy Pictures, MGM/UA Entertainment Co., United Artists Corporation, Paramount Pictures Corporation, Twentieth Century Fox Film Corporation, Universal City Studios, Inc., Walt Disney Productions, Inc., Buena Vista Distribution Co., Inc., and Warner Bros., Inc., appellees

V.

Aveco, Inc., individually and d.b.a. Nickelodeon Video Showcase and as American Video Exchange, and John P. Leonardos, individually and d.b.a. Nickelodeon Video Showcase and as American Video Exchange, appellants.

Edward W. Goebel, Jr., and Russell S. Warner of MacDonald, Illig, Jones & Britton, Erie, Pa., for the appellants. David Ladd, David E. Leibowitz, and Bruce G. Joseph of Wiley & Rein, Washington, D.C., and Burton H. Hanft and Harvey Shapiro of Sargoy, Stein & Hanft, New York City, and Lee C. Swartz of Hepford, Swartz, Menaker & Morgan, Harrisburg Pa., for the appelees.

In the U.S. Court of Appeals for the Third Circuit No. 85-5608. Dated September 4, 1986. Appeal from the U.S. District Court for the Middle District of Pennsylvania, Scranton.

Before Gibbons, Becker, and Stapleton, Circuit Judges.

Stapleton, Circuit Judge: Plaintiffs, appellees in this action, are producers of motion pictures ("Producers") and bring this copyright infringement action against the defendant, Aveco, Inc. Producers claim that Aveco's business, which includes renting video cassettes of motion pictures in conjunction with rooms in which they may be viewed, violates their exclusive rights under the Copyright Act of 1976, 17, U.S.C. Sect. 101 et seq. The district court agreed and we affirm. Jurisdiction below was predicated on 28 U.S.C. Sects. 1331 and 1338(a).

After discovery, the parties filed cross motions for summary judgment. The district court found that Aveco had infringed on Producers' exclusive rights to publicly perform and authorize public performances of their copyrighted works and so granted their motion for partial summary judgment. *Columbia Pictures Industries, Inc. v. Aveco, Inc.*, 612 F.Sup. 315 (M.D. Pa. 1985). As a result, the court entered a permanent injunction order against Aveco.[1] The parties agree that this court must exercise plenary review, as there are no disputes of material fact and the question presented is one of interpreting the relevant law. *Chrysler Credit Corp. v. First National Bank and Trust Co. of Washington*, 745 F.2d 200, 202 (3d Cir. 1984).

I

Among their other operations, Producers distribute video cassette copies of motion pictures in which they own registered copyrights. They do so knowing that many retail purchasers of these video cassettes, including Aveco, rent them to others for profit. Aveco also makes available private rooms of various sizes in which its customers may view the video cassettes that they have chosen from Aveco's offerings. For example, at one location, Lock Haven, Aveco has thirty viewing rooms, each containing seating, a video cassette player, and television monitor. Aveco charges a rental fee for the viewing room that is separate from the charge for the video cassette rental.

Customers of Aveco may (1) rent a room and also rent a video cassette for viewing in that room, (2) rent a room and bring a video cassette obtained elsewhere to play in the room, or (3) rent a video cassette for out-of-store viewing.

Aveco has placed its video cassette players inside the individual viewing rooms and, subject to a time limitation, allows the customer complete control over the playing of the video cassettes. Customers operate the video cassette players in each viewing room and Aveco's employees assist only upon request. Each video cassette may be viewed only from inside the viewing room, and is not transmitted beyond the particular room in which it is being played. Aveco asserts that it rents its viewing rooms to individual customers who may be joined in the room only by members of their families and social acquaintances. Furthermore, Aveco's stated practice is not to permit unrelated groups of customers to share a viewing room while a video cassette is being played. For purposes of this appeal we assume the veracity of these assertions.

II

As owners of copyrights in motion pictures, Producers possess statutory rights under the Copyright Act of 1976, 17, U.S.C., Sects. 101-810. Among these rights are the exclusive rights set out in Section 106 and reproduced in the margin.[2] Producers do not, in the present litigation, allege infringement of their exclusive rights "to do and to authorize [the distribution of] copies or phonorecords of the copyrighted work to the public by sale or other transfer of ownership, or by rental, lease, or lending." Thus, Aveco's rental of videocassettes for at-home viewing is not challenged.

Producers' claim in this litigation is based on the alleged infringement of their "exclusive right . . . to perform the copyrighted work publicly" and to "authorize" such performances. Producers assert that Aveco by renting its viewing rooms to the public for the purpose of watching Producers' video cassettes, is authorizing the public performance of copyrighted motion pictures.

Our analysis begins with the language of the Act. We first observe that there is no question that "performances" of copyrighted materials take place at Aveco's stores. "To perform" a work is defined in the Act as, "in the case of a motion picture or other audiovisual work to show its images in any sequence or to make the sounds accompanying it audible." Section 101. As the House Report notes, this definition means that an individual is performing a work whenever he does anything by which the work is transmitted, repeated, or made to recur. H.R. Rep. No. 1476, 94th Cong., 2d Sess. 63, *reprinted in* 1976 U.S. Code Cong. & Ad News 5659, 5676-77.

Producers do not argue that Aveco itself performs the video cassettes. They acknowledge that under the Act Aveco's *customers* are the ones performing the works, for it is they who actually place the video cassette in the video cassette player and operate the controls. As we said in *Columbia Pictures Industries* v. *Redd Horne*, 749 F.2d 154, 158 (3d Cir. 1984). "[p]laying a video cassette . . . constitute[s] a performance under Section 101." However, if there is a public performance, Aveco may still be responsible as an infringer even though it does not actually operate the video cassette players. In granting copyright owners the exclusive rights to "authorize" public performances, Congress intended "to avoid any questions as to the liability of contributory infringers. For example, a person who lawfully acquires an authorized copy of a motion picture would be an infringer if he or she engages in the business or renting it to others for purposes of an unauthorized public performance." H.R. Rep. No. 1476, 94th Cong., 2d Sess. 61, *reprinted in* 1976 U.S. Code Cong. & Ad. News at 5674; *see* S.Rep., No. 473, 94th Cong., 1st Sess. 57 (1975). In our opinion, this rationale applies equally to the person who knowingly makes available other requisites of a public performance. Accordingly, we agree with the district court that Aveco, by enabling its customers to perform the video cassettes in the viewing rooms, authorizes the performances.[3]

The performances of the Producers' motion pictures at Aveco' stores infringe their copyrights, however, only if they are "public." The copyright owners' rights do not extend to control over private performances. The Act defines a public performance.

To perform . . . a work "publicly" means —

(1) to perform or display it at a place open to the public or at any place where a substantial number of persons outside of a normal circle of a family and its social acquaintances are gathered; or

(2) to transmit or otherwise communicate a performance or display of the work to a place specified by clause (1) or to the public, by means of any device or process, whether the members of the public capable of receiving the performance or display receive it in the same place or in separate places and at the same or at different times. 17 U.S.C. Sect. 101.

We recently parsed this definition in *Redd Horne*, a case similar to the one at bar. The principal factual distinction is that in Redd Horne's operation, known as Maxwell's Video Showcase, Ltd. ("Maxwell's), the video cassette players were located in the stores' central areas, not in each individual screening room. Maxwell's customers would select a video cassette from Maxwell's stock and rent a room which they entered to watch the motion picture on a television monitor. A Maxwell's employee would play the video cassette for the customers in one of the centrally-located video cassette players and transmit the performance to the monitor located in the room. Thus, unlike Aveco's customers Maxwell's clientele had no control over the video cassette players.

The *Redd Horne* court began its analysis with the observation that the components of clause (1) of the definition of a public performance are disjunctive. 749 F.2d at 159. "The first category is self-evident; it is [']a place open to the public.' The second category, commonly referred to a semi-public place, is determined by the size and composition of the audience." *Id.*

The court then concluded that the performances were occurring at a place open to the public, which it found to be the entire store, including the viewing rooms.

Any member of the public can view a motion picture by paying the appropriate fee. The services provided by Maxwell's are essentially the same as a movie theatre, with the additional feature of privacy. The relevant "place" within the meaning of Section 101 is each of Maxwell's two stores, not each individual booth within each store. Simply because the cassettes can be viewed in private does not mitigate the essential fact that Maxwell's is unquestionably open to the public. 749 F.2d at 159.

The *Redd Horne* court reached this conclusion despite the fact that when a customer watched a movie at Maxwell's, the viewing room was closed to other members of the public. Nevertheless, Aveco asserts that factual differences between Maxwell's stores and its own require a different result in this case.

Aveco first observes that when Maxwell's employees "performed" the video cassettes they did so in a central location, the store's main area. This lobby was undeniably "open to the public." Aveco suggests that, in *Redd Horne*, the location of the customers in the private rooms was simply irrelevant, for the *performers* were in a public place, the lobby. In the case at bar, Aveco continues, its employees do not perform anything, the customers do. Unlike Maxwell's employees located in the public lobby, Aveco's customers are in private screening rooms. Aveco argues that while these viewing rooms are available to anyone for rent, they are private during each rental period, and therefore, not "open to the public." The performance—the playing of the video cassette—thus occurs not in the public lobby, but in the private viewing rooms.

We disagree. The necessary implications of Aveco's analysis is that *Redd Horne* would have been decided differently had Maxwell's located its video cassette players in a locked closet in the back of the stores. We do not read *Redd Horne* to adopt such an analysis. The Copyright Act speaks of performances at a place open to the public. It does not require that the public place be actually crowded with people. A telephone booth, a taxi cab, and even a pay toilet are commonly regarded as "open to the public," even though they are usually occupied only by one party at a time. Our opinion in *Redd Horne* turned not on the precise whereabouts of the video cassette players, but on the nature of Maxwell's stores. Maxwell's, like Aveco, was willing to make a viewing room and video cassette available to any member of the public with the inclination to avail himself of this service. It is this availability that made Maxwell's stores public places, not the coincidence that the video cassette players were situated in the lobby. Because we find *Redd Horne* indistinguishable from the case at bar, we find that Aveco's operations constituted an authorization of public performances of Producers' copyrighted works.

Aveco's reliance on the first sale doctrine is likewise misplaced. the first sale doctrine codified at 17 U.S.C. Sect. 109(a), prevents the copyright owner from controlling future transfers of a particular copy of a copyrighted work after he has transferred its "material ownership" to another. *Redd Horne*, 749 F.2d at 159. When a copyright owner parts with title to a particular copy of his copyrighted work, he thereby divests himself of his exclusive right to vend that particular copy. *Id. See United States* v. *Powell*, 701 F.2d 70, 72 (8th Cir. 1983); *United States* v. *Moore*, 604 F.2d 1228, 1232 (9th Cir. 1979). Accordingly, under the first sale doctrine, Producers cannot claim that Aveco's rentals or sales of lawfully acquired video cassettes infringe on their exclusive rights to vend those cassettes.

However, in *Redd Horne*, we found that, because of the limited control the customer had over the video cassette, Maxwell's had not actually rented or transferred the ownership in the cassette to its customers. Because we found that there had not been a "future transfer," there was no opportunity to even apply the first sale doctrine.

In the case at bar, even assuming, *arguendo*, both a waiver by Producers of their Section 106(3) distribution rights and a valid transfer of ownership of the video cassette during the rental period, the first sale doctrine is nonetheless irrelevant. The rights protected by copyright are divisible and the waiver of one does not necessarily waive any of the others. *See Section 202.*[4] In particular, the transfer of ownership in a particular copy of a work does not affect Producers' Section 106(4) exclusive rights to do and to authorize public performances. *Redd Horne*, 749 F.2d at 160; *Powell*, 701 F.2d at 72; *Moore*, 604 F.2d at 1232. It therefore cannot protect one who is infringing producers' Section 106(4) rights by the public performance of the copyrighted work.

III

We therefore conclude that Aveco, by renting its rooms to members of the general public in which they may view performances of Producers' copyrighted videocassettes, obtained from any source, has authorized public performances of those cassettes. This is a violation of Producers' Section 106 rights and is appropriately enjoined. We therefore will affirm the order of the district court.[5]

NOTES

1. The district court "permanently enjoined [Defendants] from performing or authorizing others to perform copyrighted motion pictures owned by the Plaintiffs at any place open to the public which is owned or operated by the defenants without authority or permission of the plaintiffs."

2. Section 106 states: Subject to section 107 through 118, the owner of copyright under this title has the exclusive rights to do and to authorize any of the following:

(1) to reproduce the copyrighted work in copies or phonorecords;

(2) to prepare derivative works based upon the copyrighted work;

(3) to distribute copies or phonorecords of the copyrighted work to the public by sale or other transfer of ownership, or by rental, lease, or lending;

(4) in the case of literary, musical, dramatic, and choreographic works, pantomimes, and motion pictures and other audiovisual works, to perform the copyrighted work publicly; and

(5) in the case of literary, musical, dramatic, and choreographic works, pantomimes, and pictorial, graphic, or sculptural works, including the individual images of a motion picture or other audiovisual work, to display the copyrighted work publicly. 17 U.S.C. Sect. 106.

3. Aveco authorizes the performances that occur in the viewing rooms no less when the copyrighted video cassette is obtained from some other source. Aveco encourages the public to make use of its facilities for the purpose of viewing such tapes and makes available its rooms and equipment to customers who bring cassettes with them. By thus knowingly promoting and facilitating public performances of Producers' works, Aveco authorizes those performances even when it is not the source of Producers' copyrighted video cassettes. *RCA Records* v. *All-Fast Systems, Inc.*, 594 F.Supp. 335 (S.D.N.Y. 1984) (provisions of facilities used for unlawful copying enjoined as an infringement): *Italian Book Corp.* v. *Palms Sheepshead Country Club, Inc.*, 186 U.S.P.Q. 326 (E.D.N.Y 1975).

4. Section 202 states: Ownership of a copyright, or any of the exclusive rights under a copyright, is distinct from ownership of any material object in which the work is em-

bodied. Transfer of ownership of any material object, including the copy or phonorecord in which the work is first fixed, does not of itself convey any rights in the copyrighted work embodied in the object; nor, in the absence of an agreement, does transfer of ownership of a copyright or of any exclusive rights under a copyright convey property rights in any material object. 17 U.S.C. Sect. 202.

5. Aveco argues that the injunction is impermissibly overbroad in outlawing the rental of rooms to customers for the purpose of viewing Producers' video cassettes obtained elsewhere. We agree that the injunction forbids such activity, but not that it is overbroad. See n. 3, *supra*.

APPENDIX E

TEXT OF H.R. 2429

100th Congress
1st Session

H. R. 2429

To Amend title 17, United States Code, to allow the performance of audiovisual works for inpatients in health care facilities.

IN THE HOUSE OF REPRESENTATIVES

May 14, 1987

Mr. Glickman (for himself, Mr. Synar, Mr. Cardin, and Mr. Hyde) introduced the following bill; which was referred to the Committee on the Judiciary.

A Bill

To amend title 17, United States code, to allow the performance of audiovisual works for inpatients in health care facilities.

Be it enacted by the Senate and House of Representatives of the United States of America in Congress assembled,

Section 1. Short title.

This act may be cited as the "Patients' Viewing Rights Act".

Sect. 2. Exemption for certain displays.

Chapter 1 of title 17, United States Code, is amended by adding at the end of the following new section:

Sect. 119. Limitation on exclusive rights: Performances in health care facilities

(a) Exemption. — Notwithstanding the provisions of section 106, it is not an infringement of copyright to perform a motion picture, other audiovisual work, or transmission program, before an impatient or group of inpatients in a health care facility, if —

(1) the performance is made without any purpose of direct or indirect commercial advantage and without payment of any fee or other compensation for the performance; and

(2) the performance, or the equipment used to perform, the work (other than a television from which the work is viewed), is not provided by the hospital, either directly or through a contractual or other arrangement.

(b) Definitions. — As used in this section, the term 'health care facility' means —

(1) an institution meeting the requirements of paragraphs (1) and (7) of section 1861(e) of the Social Security Act (42 U.S.C. 1395x(e)(1) and (7));

(2) an inpatient facility which —

(A) is primarily engaged in providing to individuals, on a regular basis, health or health-related care and services; and

(B) in the case of a facility in any State in which State or applicable local law provides for the licensing of facilities of this nature—

(i) is licensed pursuant to such law, or

(ii) is approved, by the agency of such State or locality responsible for licensing facilities of this nature, as meeting the standards established for such licensing; and

(C) an inpatient facility operating a hospice program meeting the requirements set forth in section 1861(dd)(2) of the Social Security Act (42 U.S.C. 1395x(dd)(2)).

Sec. 3. Technical amendments.

(a) Cross Reference.—Section 106 of title 17, United States Code, is amended by striking out "118" and inserting in lieu thereof "119".

(b) Table of Sections.—The table of sections at the beginning of chapter 1 of title 17, United States Code, is amended by adding at the end the following:

"119. Limitations on exclusive rights. Performances in health care facilities."

CURRENT AND FORTHCOMING PUBLICATIONS FROM COPYRIGHT INFORMATION SERVICES

Sinofsky, E.R., *A Copyright Primer for Educational and Industrial Media Producers*. 1988.
> A copyright guide for film, video, and multi-image producers.

Strong, W.S., *The Copyright Book: A Practical Guide*, Second ed. 1984. $13.95.
> A copyright guide for authors, artists, photographers, etc.

Talab, R.S., *Commonsense Copyright: A Guide to the New Technologies*. 1985. $14.95.
> Applies the copyright law to all types of instructional hardware, from photocopiers to computer networks.

Vlcek, C.W., *Copyright Policy Development: A Resource Book for Educators*. 1987. $17.95.
> A handbook for writing school and college copyright policies. Includes sample policies which may be modified and adopted.

Official Fair-use Guidelines: Complete Texts of Four Official Documents Arranged for Use by Educators. 3d ed. 1987. $5.95. Discounts on sales of two or more copies.
> Includes the Congressional fair-use guidelines, plus the 1987 ICCA computer copyright guidelines.

Miller, J.K., *Computer/Copyright Seminar*, 1988. [audio cassette and documents.] 1988, $24.88.
> Treats copyright issues facing educational computer users. The new ICCA copyright guidelines are included and discussed.

Miller, J.K., *The Copyright Directory, Vol. l: General Information.* 1985. $23; $5 discount to nonprofit libraries.
> Provides names, addresses, and phone numbers of thousands of individuals and organizations involved in the copyright law.

Miller, J.K., *Church/Copyright Seminar*, 1987. [audio cassette and documents.] 1987. $24.87.
> Treats video and music copyright issues facing church workers. Includes the new NCC video guidelines.

Miller, J.K., *Video/Copyright Seminar*, 1988. [audio cassette and documents.] 1988, $24.88.
> Treats videotaping off the air and off the satellite, using videocassettes in school and college settings, etc.

Miller, J.K. (Ed.), *Video Copyright Permissions*, 1988, price not established.
> Provides practical information about securing licenses and establishing procedures for duplicating and transmitting video materials.

Add $1.50 per order for shipping and handling.

INDEX

PERSONAL NOTES

USING COPYRIGHTED VIDEOCASSETTES